D0624447

MICROWAVE COOKBOOK

Recipes developed using Sharp Carousel Microwave Ovens from 700
to 1050 watts. The minimum cooking times are appropriate for higher
wattage ovens and the maximum cooking times are appropriate for lower
wattage ovens. Check operation manual for the wattage of your oven.

HOW TO USE THIS COOKBOOK

Your Sharp Carousel Convection Microwave Oven can be used as a microwave oven for quick, convenient cooking, as a convection oven for small baked goods and broiling or in combination for roasting and baking.

Your cookbook begins with an introduction to the principles and techniques of microwave cooking, pages 4-24. The next section, pages 1c through 48c, explains convection and combination cooking and includes cooking methods, charts and recipes. The chapters following page 48c focus on microwave-only cooking.

Notice that any recipe listed in the index with a "c" following the page number is a convection or combination recipe. This is a quick way of identifying convection or combination recipes.

For some foods you will find directions for both combination cooking (1c-48c) and microwave cooking. For example, you'll find directions for baking cakes in combination on page 30c, and a recipe for microwaving layer cakes on page 107. Your oven provides you with the option of using either method, depending on the time you have available and your own preferences.

Take a moment to flip through the cookbook to see how it's arranged. As you use the book, be sure to read the captions under the pictures — often that's where you'll find important directions and tips.

PRECAUTIONS TO AVOID POSSIBLE EXPOSURE TO EXCESSIVE MICROWAVE ENERGY

(a) Do not attempt to operate this oven with the door open since open-door operation can result in harmful exposure to microwave energy. It is important not to defeat or tamper with the safety interlocks.

(b) Do not place any object between the oven front face and the door or allow soil or cleaner residue to accumulate on sealing surfaces.

(c) Do not operate the oven if it is damaged. It is particularly important that the oven door close properly and that there is no damage to the: (1) door (bent), (2) hinges and latches (broken or loosened), (3) door seals and sealing surfaces.

(d) The oven should not be adjusted or repaired by anyone except properly qualified service personnel.

Design & Production: Cy DeCosse Incorporated

CONTENTS

How a Microwave Oven Works

Once you've become familiar with your microwave oven, you'll soon discover it will make your work in the kitchen easier and more efficient. Included in this book are recipes plus many tips and techniques. Be sure to read the operation manual that accompanies your oven for specific recommendations.

Advantages of the Carousel

Sharp Carousel Microwave Ovens are designed with a revolving turntable featuring advanced technology. This remarkable system makes sure food is cooked evenly and thoroughly without hot or cold spots. Since the energy in a microwave oven often is not distributed evenly throughout the cavity, the turntable moves the food through any hot spots. There's no need for you to rotate food to achieve best results.

Once you've become familiar with your microwave oven, you'll soon discover it will make your work in the kitchen easier and more efficient. Included in this book are recipes developed for 700 to 1050 watt ovens, plus many tips and techniques. Be sure to read the operation manual that accompanies your oven for specific recommendations.

Microwave Myths

Learning what is fact and what is fiction will help you understand how your microwave oven works and what it can do for you.

Myth 1. Microwaves cook from the inside out.

Actually, it's the reverse. Food prepared in a microwave oven cooks from the outside toward the center. Microwaves penetrate the food from the outside edges to a depth of about 3/4 to 1 1/2 inches. Small foods, under 2 inches in diameter, heat more quickly because the microwaves penetrate from all sides. With larger foods, heat moves to the center by conduction.

Myth 2. You can't use metal in a microwave oven.

There are exceptions to the rule of "no metal in a microwave oven." Metal reflects microwave energy, which slows cooking. Small strips of aluminum foil may be used to shield areas of food to keep them from overcooking. (See page 12 for further information.) The use of metal twist ties, pots and pans or metal utensils is not recommended, because they could cause arcing (energy trapped between oven wall and metal, creating blue flashes). Always be sure to check your operation manual for specific recommendations.

Myth 3. Dishes don't get hot in a microwave oven.

Some microwave-safe dishes become hot because they absorb heat from contact with hot food. This is often the case when food is tightly covered during periods of longer cooking.

Myth 4. Microwaved foods don't stay hot.

They cool at the same rate as conventionally heated foods. One advantage of microwaving is that you can cook and serve in the same dish; food stays hot longer because you don't have to transfer it to a cool dish.

Myth 5. Foods don't brown in a microwave oven.

Browning depends on fat content and the amount of cooking time in relation to food volume. Foods such as bacon, turkey or a roast will brown. Many small, moist foods cook so quickly they don't have time to brown.

Do's and Don'ts

Humidity and moisture in food influence the amount of condensation in your oven. This is normal in microwave cooking. Be sure the vent on the back of oven is not blocked. The door seal on your oven is designed to prevent leakage of microwave energy during cooking. Moisture that may occasionally appear around the oven door is normal.

Here are a few do's and don'ts that will start you on your way to learning more about your microwave oven:

Do read the operation manual that accompanies your oven for specific recommendations.

Do follow manufacturer's recommendations for oven cooking bags. Make six ½-inch slits in neck of bag below tie to allow steam to escape during cooking.

Do use small amounts of foil to shield and protect portions of meat and poultry from overcooking; be sure to keep foil at least 2 inches from oven walls and ceiling.

Do pop popcorn only in a microwave popcorn popper or use specially packaged ready-to-pop microwave popcorn. Some ovens include a special feature for popping popcorn. (See operation manual for further information.) Do not use brown paper bags or glass or plastic bowls for popping popcorn.

Do not dry herbs, wood, gourds or wet papers in the microwave oven.

Do prick foods with skins, such as potatoes or squash, so internal steam that builds up during cooking can escape.

Do read recipes for dish size and shape, to ensure that they will fit into your microwave oven.

Do cover meat and poultry with wax paper or vented plastic wrap. Remember to turn over or rearrange halfway through cooking time for even cooking results.

Do hard-poach eggs for salads and casseroles; prick yolk to allow steam to escape. **Do not** cook eggs in the shell or reheat unpeeled hard-cooked eggs in the microwave oven.

Do not use your microwave oven to heat oil or fat for deep-frying. **Do not** can foods in the microwave oven.

Microwave Utensils

The ideal material for a microwave utensil allows energy to pass through the container and heat the food. Many common household items, such as paper plates and glass or plastic bowls, are good choices for warming foods.

When a utensil is used for cooking, it must also be able to withstand contact with hot food or boiling liquid.

Dual-purpose, heat-resistant paper and plastic utensils can be used in microwave and conventional ovens. Look for materials that are marked "safe for microwave or conventional oven up to 400°F." Many traditional cooking containers, such as casseroles and measuring cups, are also suitable for microwaving.

Oven-glass and glass ceramic (Pyroceram®) utensils can be used for microwaving, serving and storing. Oven-glass utensils are inexpensive and widely available. Use them for measuring, mixing and microwaving. Choose clear glass for pies, cakes and breads, so you can easily check for doneness through the bottom of the dish.

Microwave-safe Dish Test. If you are not sure whether your dish is safe to use in the microwave oven, use this test. Place the dish in the oven. Measure ½ to 1 cup water in glass cup. Place on or beside dish. Microwave at HIGH (100%) for 1 to 2 minutes. If dish remains cool, it is suitable for microwaving. Do not use this test for plastic.

Pottery, stoneware and porcelain offer the convenience of cook-and-serve versatility. Serving bowls, platters, casseroles, plates and cups are practical and attractive. Look for dishware that is marked "microwave-safe". If you are not sure if your dish is safe to use, use the dish test above.

Plastic cookware (Thermoset®) marked microwave-safe is designed for microwave oven and conventional oven use and can withstand temperatures up to 400°F. Follow manufacturer's recommendations.

Plastic storage containers and tableware marked "dishwasher-safe" and Styrofoam® may be used for short-term heating to serving temperature. Do not use them for cooking raw foods or for heating foods high in fat or sugar, since they distort at fairly low temperatures. "Original" Tupperware® may melt or distort; Ultra 21® lines from Tupperware are designed for microwave use.

Plastic wrap and oven cooking bags are ideal for microwaving. Plastic food-storage bags should not be used for cooking. Plastic wrap makes a convenient cover for baking dishes; vent so steam escapes. Choose a good-quality plastic wrap or one designed for microwave use; inferior brands may split, become sticky or shrink when used.

Paper plates, hot drink cups, towels and napkins are good choices for short-term cooking and heating. Avoid recycled paper, which may contain metal chips, and wax-coated paper cups or plates. Paper baking cups absorb excess moisture and save clean-ups. Plain white paper towels are excellent for warming breads, cooking bacon or covering to prevent splatters. Wax paper can be used as a light, nonstick cover that holds in steam; it also prevents splattering for dishes such as chili or spaghetti.

Dual-purpose paper products, such as ovenable paperboard containers, are versatile choices. They are freezer-proof and safe for both microwave and conventional ovens up to 400°F.

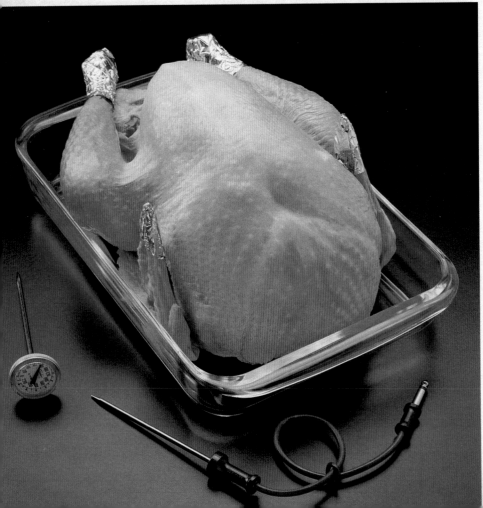

Metal, such as small pieces of aluminum foil, may be used to shield small areas of food (wingtips, leg ends, breast bones) from overcooking and overdefrosting. Metal reflects energy away from food and slows cooking. Special microwave thermometers designed to be left in the oven during cooking and temperature probes are also valuable tools. Shallow (no more than 1¾ inches in depth) foil convenience-food trays may be used. The amount of metal used must be in proportion to the volume of food; foil trays should be two-thirds to three-fourths full. Always keep metal at least 2 inches away from oven walls and ceiling to prevent arcing.

Special Microwave Accessories

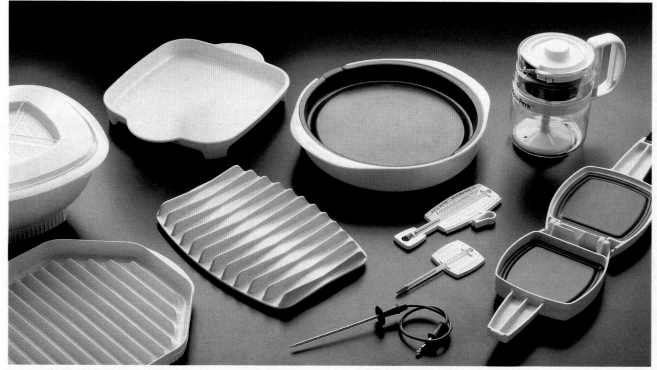

Browning dishes and skillets make it easy to sear, brown or crisp foods such as steaks, hamburgers or chops in the microwave oven.

Microwave sandwich grills make it easy to cook and brown a single hamburger or grill a cheese sandwich. Follow manufacturer's instructions for preheating and cooking times.

Microwave popcorn poppers make it fast, easy and safe to pop fresh popcorn. Follow manufacturer's instructions for use.

Microwave coffee makers allow you to prepare two or four cups of freshly brewed coffee in minimum time.

Microwave thermometers and temperature probes are handy for microwave cooking. Instant-read thermometers, microwave meat thermometers and candy thermometers are ideal for testing temperature of meats, poultry, casseroles, soups and candies. Microwave meat and candy thermometers can be left in the microwave oven during cooking. Some instant-read thermometers can only be used outside the microwave oven. Some ovens are equipped with temperature probes. See page 16 or operation manual for further information.

Roasting racks and bacon racks elevate meats during microwaving so they do not steam in fat and juices.

Not Recommended for Use in the Microwave Oven

Do not use metal pots, pans or bakeware, metal twist ties or dishes with metallic trim. Also avoid utensils with metal screws, bands or handles, metal reinforcement in some baskets or wicker-wrapped handles and conventional meat or candy thermometers. Melamine® or Centura® tableware, plastics that may be sensitive to hot foods, leaded crystal, antique or delicate glassware, fine bone china and ceramic mugs or cups with glued-on handles, brown paper bags and recycled paper products are not recommended for any microwave cooking use.

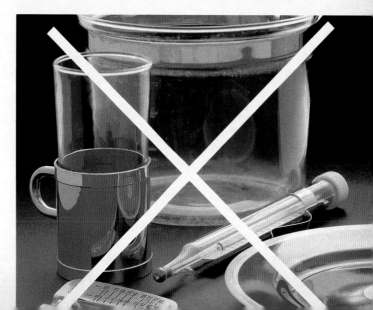

Microwave Cooking Principles

The key to successful microwave cooking is understanding the basic conditions which may affect cooking results. The speed and evenness of microwave cooking are influenced by characteristics of the food itself and by differences in line voltage. House power varies throughout the country. Voltage fluctuates and is lower during periods of peak consumption.

Microwaves penetrate foods to a depth of about ¾ to 1½ inches on all surfaces: top, bottom and sides. The interior of foods greater than 2 inches in diameter heats by conduction, as it does in conventional cooking. Foods with high water, fat or sugar content respond quickly to microwave energy.

Quantity. Small amounts cook faster than large ones. Microwaving time is always directly related to the amount of food and increases with the quantity. When doubling a recipe, increase time by about one-half and check for doneness.

Size. Small pieces cook faster than large ones. To speed cooking, cut pieces smaller than 2 inches so microwaves can penetrate to the center from all sides. For even cooking, cut vegetables, fruit and meat into pieces of uniform size.

Shape. Foods which are irregular in shape, like fish fillets, chicken breasts or drumsticks, take longer to cook in the thicker parts. To help them cook evenly, place the thickest parts to the outside of the dish, where they will receive more energy.

Starting temperature. Frozen or refrigerated food takes longer to heat than food at room temperature. Cooking times in this book are based on normal storage temperatures. Since rooms, refrigerators and freezers differ in temperature, check for doneness at the minimum time.

Moisture content. Microwaves are readily attracted to moisture. Naturally moist foods microwave better than dry ones. Add a minimum of liquid to moist foods, as excess water slows cooking.

Fat and bone. Marbling within meat or a thin, even layer of fat on a roast attracts energy and speeds cooking. Drain excess drippings in dish during cooking to speed cooking. Bone conducts heat, so areas next to it may cook faster than other areas.

Density. Porous foods, such as ground beef or mashed potatoes, cook faster than dense foods, such as steak or whole potatoes, since microwaves penetrate them more easily. Turn dense foods over after one-half cooking time to speed and equalize cooking.

Microwave Cooking Techniques

Many of the techniques of microwaving are similar to those used in conventional cooking. They help equalize energy in the food so that it cooks evenly and quickly, allowing you the full benefit of microwave speed.

Dish shapes and sizes affect the way foods cook, the amount of attention they require during cooking and the speed at which they cook. The depth of the container is a key to success. Food in a shallow casserole will cook faster than food in a deep dish of the same capacity. Avoid casseroles with sloping sides. A straight-sided casserole keeps the depth of food uniform for even cooking. Whenever possible, choose round dishes. Square or rectangular dishes may lead to overcooking in the corners. Ring shapes are excellent for foods that cannot be stirred during microwaving.

Shielding is a useful technique that protects sensitive areas of food from overcooking. Use small strips of aluminum foil on the wing tips, ends of drumsticks or the breastbone of a turkey, top or edges of a roast, or corners of a square cake or a pan of bar cookies. These small pieces of foil reflect microwave energy away from the food, acting as a protective shield. Heat transfer from other areas of the food cooks shielded areas. Keep foil at least 2 inches from oven walls and ceiling. Covering meats with a sauce also acts as a shield to prevent drying.

Covering

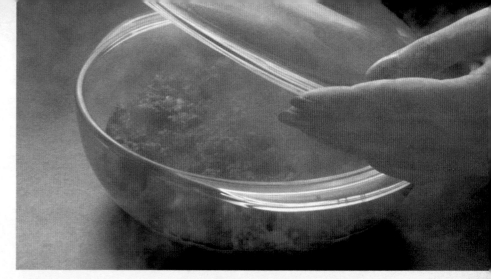

Glass lids will hold in steam to tenderize food, keep moisture in and speed cooking.

Plastic wrap holds in steam to speed cooking and tenderize food. Vent by turning back one edge to form a narrow slot for steam to escape. A tight, unvented plastic cover may split during cooking. Always remove plastic cover away from yourself to prevent steam burns.

Wax paper forms a loose, nonstick cover similar to "partial covering" in conventional cooking. Use it to hold in heat, speed cooking and prevent splatters with foods that do not need to steam.

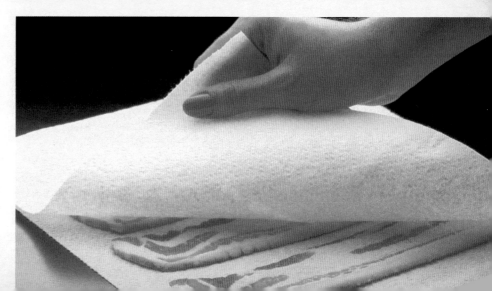

Paper towels allow steam to escape while they prevent splatters and absorb excess moisture. They are excellent for covering bacon or foods that tend to splatter. Napkins and paper towels are also good for warming bread or rolls. Choose plain white napkins and paper towels. Avoid paper products with heavy dyes and prints.

Microwave Cooking Techniques (continued)

Arrange foods such as individual meat loaves and baking potatoes in a ring around the outside of turntable spacing at least 1 inch apart so energy can penetrate from top and sides.

Turn foods over once during microwaving to speed cooking of medium-size pieces, such as chicken or hamburgers. Large items, such as a turkey, roast or whole cauliflower, should be turned over during cooking time to speed and equalize cooking.

Rearrange closely packed foods, such as meatballs, during cooking, so pieces from the outside are moved to the center. Tuck thin ends of fish fillets under for more even cooking.

Stir foods such as casseroles, vegetables, soups and sauces from the outside to the center of dish once or twice during cooking to equalize heat and speed microwaving. Foods will not scorch or stick, so there's no need to stir constantly as you do in conventional cooking.

Standing time allows food to complete cooking after it is removed from the oven. Since heat is in the food, not the microwave oven, many foods build up enough internal heat so that they continue to cook by themselves. It is important to let roasts, cakes and whole vegetables stand to finish cooking. This will allow the centers to be done without overcooking or drying the outsides.

Standing time can range from 1 to 15 minutes. Recipes direct slight undercooking to compensate for standing times. Tent roasts with foil during standing time. Internal temperature will rise 10 to 20°F. during standing. Cakes will appear moist on top surface, but when they are allowed to stand directly on countertop, heat is trapped and finishes the cooking.

Browning develops on roasts and turkeys or on chops, steaks and hamburgers microwaved in a browning utensil. Many foods cook so quickly in the microwave oven, they do not have time to brown. For meats and poultry, use melted butter, soy, Worcestershire, barbecue or steak sauce to add color and flavor.

A sprinkling of paprika or dry gravy mix, jelly glaze or a crumb coating also gives a browned appearance. Casseroles can be topped at the end of microwaving with grated cheese or crumbs. Finish cakes and breads with frostings or toppings or grease the cake dish and coat it with graham cracker crumbs.

Microwave Cooking Techniques: Doneness Tests

Many techniques for testing doneness are the same as the ones you use for conventional cooking. One key difference is learning to let standing time finish cooking microwaved foods.

Cook meats to their proper internal temperatures. See chart on pages 36 and 37 for removal and temperatures after standing. Casseroles, soups and stews should be at least 165°F. when removed from the oven.

Fish flakes easily with fork when done. The center is slightly translucent but continues to cook during standing time. Fish toughens and dries if overcooked.

Test cake for doneness by inserting wooden pick in center. If the pick comes out clean and the edges pull away from the dish, cake is done. Let stand directly on countertop to trap heat. Small moist spots on surface will finish cooking during standing time.

Using Temperature Probes

A good way to eliminate guesswork when testing for doneness is to use a temperature probe. If your oven comes with a temperature probe, use it to cook foods such as roasts, casseroles, soups and hot drinks to a given temperature. The probe shuts the oven off automatically when food reaches a preset internal temperature. The tip of the probe should be inserted in the center of the food at least two-thirds of its length. Insert temperature probe in roasts at the center of the meatiest portion, not touching bone or fat. Boneless cuts of pork are advised. For casseroles, soups or beverages, you may want to support the probe by covering casserole with two sheets of plastic wrap, slightly overlapping at center. Insert probe at center where plastic wrap meets.

Recipe Conversion

Many conventional recipes can be converted simply by cutting back on cooking time. The best guide is a microwave recipe similar to the one being converted.

Reduce liquid in conventional recipes which call for raw ingredients, simmering or long baking times. Little evaporation occurs during microwaving, so use two-thirds the liquid and add more, if needed, as you cook.

Omit fat needed to brown foods and prevent sticking in conventional cooking. A small amount of margarine or olive oil may be used for flavor. Since many foods do not brown in the microwave oven, you may want to use a sauce or topping, such as Cheddar cheese, or a browning agent to enhance their appearance or flavor.

Use less salt, since it attracts microwave energy and draws liquid out of food. To avoid brown specks on vegetables or dry spots on meats, combine salt with a sauce or salt food after cooking. Use less of highly flavored seasonings like garlic, chili, curry powder, sage and pepper. After microwaving, correct seasoning to taste. Small amounts of mild herbs and spices need not be changed.

Reduce power level when microwaving long-cooking dense foods, such as roasts; delicate foods, like egg-based custards, quiches and cream-based sauces or high-protein foods, like cheese-based sauces and fondues. For cakes and quick breads, use lower power level initially for food to rise evenly; finish with higher power level to set structure. At reduced power levels, delicate foods won't overcook, and meats have time to cook evenly without overcooking edges.

Reheating

Reheating food is a specialty of the microwave oven. Many Sharp microwave ovens are equipped with special programmed settings or automatic sensors for reheating favorite foods. If your oven has an automatic reheat setting, check your operation manual for specific directions. For freshest-tasting results, use power levels recommended in chart, opposite.

Plates of food. Arrange food with thickest parts of meat and bulky vegetables to outside of plate and quick-to-heat less-dense foods in center. Spread single serving of a main dish in an even layer on plate. Cover with wax paper or plastic wrap. Reheat until bottom of plate feels very warm in the center. Temperature should be at least 165°F.

Pasta, rice and rolls. For leftover rice or pasta, drizzle with 1 tablespoon water per cup and reheat, covered. To reheat bread, rolls or muffins, wrap in paper towel and microwave only until warm to the touch, not piping hot. Breads heat in seconds; overheating can cause breads to become tough, dry and hard.

Meats. Medium (¼-inch) slices reheat best. Cover meat with sauce or gravy to protect from drying out. Meats with sauce should be covered with wax paper to hold in heat. Cover meat slices without gravy with paper towel.

Reheating Chart

Item	Starting Temperature	Microwave Time	Procedure
Plate of Food 1 serving of meat, 2 servings of vegetables	Room temp. Refrigerated	MED.-HIGH (70%) 1-2½ min. 2½-3½ min.	Meaty portions and bulky vegetables to outside. Cover with wax paper.
Meat (Chicken pieces, chops, hamburgers, meat loaf slices) 1 serving 2 servings	Refrigerated Refrigerated	MED.-HIGH (70%) 1-2 min. 2-4 min.	Cover loosely with wax paper.
Meat Slices (Beef, ham, pork, turkey) 1 or more servings	Room temp. Refrigerated	MEDIUM (50%) 1-1¾ min. per serving 1½-2½ min. per serving	Cover with gravy or wax paper. Check after 30 sec. per serving.
Stirrable Casseroles and Main Dishes 1 serving 2 servings 4-6 servings	Refrigerated Refrigerated Refrigerated	HIGH (100%) 1¾-3½ min. 3¾-5 min. 6½-7½ min.	Cover with plastic wrap. Stir after half the time.
Nonstirrable Casseroles and Main Dishes 1 serving 2 servings 4-6 servings	Refrigerated Refrigerated Refrigerated	MEDIUM (50%) 4½-7½ min. 7½-11 min. 12-15 min.	Cover with wax paper.
Soup, Cream 1 cup 1 can (10¾ oz.)	Refrigerated Room temp.	MEDIUM (50%) 2¾-5½ min. 5-7½ min.	Cover. Stir after half the time.
Soup, Clear 1 cup 1 can (10¾ oz.)	Refrigerated Room temp.	HIGH (100%) 1¾-3 min. 3½-4½ min.	Cover. Stir after half the time.
Pizza 1 slice 1 slice 2 slices 2 slices	Room temp. Refrigerated Room temp. Refrigerated	HIGH (100%) 15-25 sec. 25-35 sec. 25-35 sec. 35-45 sec.	Place on paper towel on microwave-safe rack.
Vegetables 1 serving 2 servings	Refrigerated Refrigerated	HIGH (100%) ¾-1¼ min. 1½-2 min.	Cover. Stir after half the time.
Baked Potato 1 2	Refrigerated Refrigerated	HIGH (100%) 1-2½ min. 2½-3 min.	Cut potato lengthwise and then several times crosswise. Cover with wax paper.
Breads (Dinner or breakfast roll) 1 roll 2 rolls 4 rolls	Room temp. Room temp. Room temp.	HIGH (100%) 8-10 sec. 10-12 sec. 15-18 sec.	Wrap single roll, bagel or muffin in paper towel. To reheat several, line plate with paper towel; cover with another paper towel.
Pie 1 slice 2 slices	Refrigerated Refrigerated	HIGH (100%) 30-45 sec. 1-1½ min.	Place on microwave-safe dish. Do not cover.

Defrosting Frozen Foods

Defrosting food with the microwave oven is not only faster than any other method, it can also give better results. Many microwave ovens are designed with a special automatic defrost setting which makes it safe, quick and easy to defrost meats and poultry. Check your operation manual for specific directions.

Once frozen meat is defrosted, it begins to lose its juices. Microwave ovens give you the advantage of letting you defrost meat just before you cook it for maximum juiciness and quality.

Microwave defrosting is easy, but some attention is needed to make sure that the ice crystals in frozen food melt without the food starting to cook. MEDIUM-LOW (30%) is fast enough to be convenient but gradual enough to give good results. At MEDIUM (50%), meat defrosts in about one-third less time but needs more attention.

Place plastic or paper-wrapped package of frozen food directly in oven. To speed defrosting, remove wrap as soon as possible and cover food with wax paper to hold in heat and prevent moisture loss. Foil wrappings must be removed.

Break up or separate ground beef, cubed meat, chicken pieces or fish fillets after one-third of defrosting time. Remove any defrosted portions and put remainder in baking dish to complete defrosting.

Turn over flat roasts, steaks, chops, whole chickens or Cornish hens after half the defrosting time. If package contains several steaks or chops, separate as soon as possible and place in baking dish.

Remove wrapping from turkey so you can feel warm spots as it defrosts. Metal clamps holding legs should be removed as soon as possible. Start breast side down, shield warm areas with small strips of foil and turn over after each one-fourth of time.

Let turkey stand 20 to 30 minutes submerged in cold water after defrosting, until giblets and neck can be removed and breast meat under wings is completely defrosted. Turkey may be microwaved with clamps if they are difficult to remove.

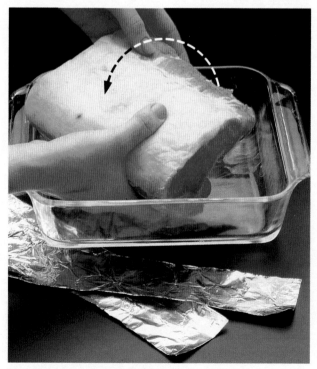

Turn over large roasts after half the defrosting time. As you turn, touch meat for warm areas and shield these with small pieces of foil. Let roasts stand 20 to 30 minutes after second half of defrosting time.

Defrost meats and poultry only until they can be pierced to the center with a skewer or wooden pick. Surface or cavity should feel cool but not icy. Cook immediately after defrosting or refrigerate until cooking time.

Defrosting Frozen Foods Chart

General procedure for defrosting: Place plastic or paper-wrapped packages of frozen food directly in oven. Remove wrappings as soon as possible then place in baking dish. Cover with wax paper. Continue defrosting.

If your microwave oven has a special automatic defrost setting, be sure to read the operation manual for recommendations and procedure.

Power Level: MEDIUM-LOW (30%)

Cut	Microwave Time	Standing Time	Special Instructions
Meats			
Ground Meat	5-10 min. per lb.	5-10 min.	Break apart, remove any defrosted pieces as soon as possible. Place remainder in baking dish.
Chops	5½-8½ min. per lb.	5-10 min.	Separate and turn over once.
Ribs	7-12 min. per lb.	10-15 min.	Separate and rearrange once.
Steaks & Flat Roasts	7-9½ min. per lb.	5-10 min.	Turn over after half the time. Shield as needed.
Thick Roasts	9½-11½ min. per lb.	20-30 min.	Turn over after half the time. Shield as needed.
Cubed Meat	8-12 min. per lb.	5-10 min.	Separate and rearrange once.
Poultry			
Whole Turkey	7½-10 min. per lb.	20-30 min.	Divide total time into 4 parts. Place breast side down in baking dish. Microwave one-fourth of total time. Turn breast side up. Microwave one-fourth of time. Shield warm spots as needed. Let stand 15 minutes. Turn turkey on side. Microwave one-fourth of time. Turn on other side. Microwave remaining time. Remove giblets. Let stand in cool water until cool but not icy, 20 to 30 minutes.
Half Turkey, Turkey Breast	7-10½ min. per lb.	15-20 min.	Breast side down. Turn over after half the time. Shield as needed. Rinse in cool water after defrosting.
Turkey Pieces	7-10½ min. per lb.	5-10 min.	Turn over after half the time. Shield as needed. Rinse in cool water after defrosting.
Whole Chicken	5-9 min. per lb.	10-20 min.	Breast side down. Turn over after half the time. Shield as needed.
Chicken Quarters, Pieces	8-11 min. per lb.	5-15 min.	Separate and rearrange once.
Boneless Breasts	7-11 min. per lb.	15-20 min.	Place on roasting rack. Microwave for half the time. Separate pieces. Microwave remaining time until pliable but cold.
Duck	8-11 min. per lb.	10-20 min.	Breast side down. Turn over after half the time. Shield as needed.
Cornish Hens	9-12 min. per lb.	5-10 min.	Breast side down. Turn over after half the time. Shield as needed.
Fish & Seafood			
Fillets & Steaks	8-10 min. per lb.	5-10 min.	Separate and rearrange once.
Whole Small Fish	7-14 min. per lb.	5-10 min.	Separate and rearrange once.
Scallops & Shrimp	5-9 min. per lb.	5 min.	Separate and rearrange once.

Convenience Foods

Most convenience foods now include microwave directions, making it easier than ever to enjoy soups, snacks, beverages, entrees and desserts. The package instructions are usually for HIGH (100%) for maximum speed and efficiency.

How to Defrost Bagels and Muffins

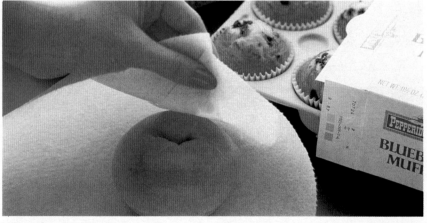

Wrap frozen bagel or muffin in a paper towel or napkin. Microwave at MEDIUM (50%) until just warm to the touch (about 25 to 45 seconds for one, 40 seconds to 1 minute 20 seconds for two). Split bagels or muffins and toast, if desired.

How to Defrost Orange Juice or Lemonade Concentrate

Remove one metal lid from 6-ounce can of frozen juice. Place can upright in oven. Microwave at HIGH (100%) 30 seconds to 1 minute 30 seconds. Concentrate should be softened but not warm. Pour into container and stir in cold water as directed on can.

How to Microwave Canned Soups

Heat condensed canned soups in a 4-cup measure, a casserole or individual serving bowls for quick clean-ups. If diluted with water, microwave soup at HIGH (100%) until hot. If diluted with milk, microwave at MEDIUM (50%) until hot.

How to Pop Popcorn

Now it's faster and easier than ever to pop fresh popcorn in your microwave oven. You can use special microwave popcorn poppers. Be sure to follow the manufacturer's simple instructions. Ready-to-pop packages of microwave popcorn offer maximum convenience. The directions are on the package. "Listen" for the popping to slow. Selected Sharp microwave ovens are equipped with a separate popcorn setting to automatically pop packaged microwave popcorn; corn is done when it stops popping. See operation manual for exact instructions.

French Fries and Other Favorites

For speedy, crisp French fries and other convenience frozen potato products, first defrost in the microwave and then place under conventional broiler or on a microwave browning tray to crisp.

CONVECTION MICROWAVE COOKBOOK

What is Convection Microwave Cooking?

The convection microwave oven is the ultimate cooking team. This state-of-the-art system brings together the best of both worlds. Enjoy the browning and crisping capabilities of convection plus the speed of microwave cooking. Microwaving brings out the natural flavor of foods and keeps them moist and juicy. Convection cooking adds the advantage of browning and crisping food beautifully. Combination settings LOW MIX and HIGH MIX use convection heat to seal and brown the outside while using microwave energy to make sure the interior is cooked.

Breads and cakes are done to perfection; roasts and poultry brown and crisp just right. The results are superior to conventional methods, giving you the widest range of options for creative cooking and timesaving ease. It is not necessary to preheat with combination settings.

When you compare foods cooked in a convection microwave oven with those cooked conventionally, you'll discover the advantages of this advanced system.

Turkey is an excellent example of the superb results you can achieve with this team. The combination oven lets you roast a larger turkey than is possible with microwaving alone. No turning over is needed, and you don't need to baste unless a special seasoning is desired. Turkey roasted conventionally browns well, but white meat often becomes dry in the time needed to cook dark meat completely. Combination settings use hot air roasting for crisp, brown skin plus microwaving speed for moist, juicy meat.

Breads and cakes also turn out beautifully. The convection microwave team bakes bread with a golden brown, crisp crust and fine texture. Cakes are tender, moist and evenly cooked with a nicely browned surface. You can also bake two layers at a time rather than the one-at-a-time method of microwave-only baking.

LOW MIX combines convection heat with microwave power for perfect baking results. Use the Low Mix setting for baked goods that require more than 20 minutes baking time. Angel food and bundt cakes, quick breads and yeast breads and large muffins are examples of foods that bake perfectly at this setting. Check owner's manual for further information.

HIGH MIX combines convection heat with microwave power, providing crisp brown exteriors and superior juiciness for meats. Longer-cooking foods, such as roasts, whole turkey and chicken and poultry pieces, cook in about half of the time with just the right amount of browning. Check owner's manual for further information.

What is Convection Cooking?

With convection cooking, a high-speed fan circulates air past the heat source and around the food. The superheated air browns and crisps the food beautifully.

Convection cooking is ideal for foods requiring 20 minutes or less cooking time. Two sheets of cookies or two pans of muffins bake at the same time, saving you time. Preheating is necessary with convection cooking. Use the convection setting for baked goods such as cookies, biscuits, cupcakes and small muffins or frozen or refrigerated convenience-food items.

What is Convection Broiling?

In convection broiling, food is elevated on the broiling trivet, allowing cooking to occur on all sides simultaneously. It is not necessary to turn foods over during cooking. Fats drip away from the food, providing for great flavor without all the fat.

Convection Broiling is easier than ever with the unique one-step programming broiling feature of Sharp Carousel II Microwave Ovens. Prepare hamburgers, chops, steaks, fish steaks and chicken pieces with ease and minimum attention.

3c

Foods and Best Cooking Methods

There's an easy way to cook each of your favorite foods. Matching the best method and setting to the food is the secret to success time after time. This chart keeps it simple by giving you the everyday guidelines you need. Now you can tell at a glance whether it's best to use the Convection or Microwave only method, the Broil setting or combination cycles of LOW MIX/Bake or HIGH MIX/Roast.

Legend: Convection ■ | Low Mix ▨ | Microwave ▢ | Broil ▫ | High Mix ◼

Food	Convection	Low Mix	High Mix	Broil	Microwave
Breads & Rolls					
Biscuits	■				
Bread Loaves		▨			
Rolls	■				
Cakes					
Bundt		▨			
Cupcakes	■				
Layer Cakes	■				
Loaf Cakes or Quick Breads		▨			
Muffins (regular size)	■				
Muffins (bakery-style, large size)		▨			
Tube Cakes		▨			
Cookies					
Bar or Brownies		▨			
All Other Cookies	■				
Defrosting					▢
Desserts					
Cheesecake		▨			
Cream Puffs or Eclairs	■				
Crisps or Cobblers		▨			
Frozen Convenience Foods					
Bake under 20 min.	■				
Bake over 20 min.		▨			

Food	Convection	Low Mix	High Mix	Broil	Microwave
Meat, Fish & Poultry					
Bacon					
Casseroles			██		
Chicken, Whole Roasting			██		
Chicken Pieces			██	░░	
Chops — Lamb, Pork, Veal				░░	
Hamburgers				░░	
Ham Steak				░░	
Hot Dogs				░░	░░
Fish & Seafood			██	░░	
Meat Loaf			██		
Roasts — Beef, Lamb, Pork, Veal			██		
Sausage				░░	
Steaks & London Broil				░░	
Turkey, Whole & Breast			██		
Pies					
Crust	██				
Custard or Pumpkin		▒▒			
Double-Crust			██		
Frozen Prepared Custard		▒▒			
Frozen Prepared Fruit			██		
Variety Pies (pecan, chess, etc.)		▒▒			
Pizza	██				
Potatoes					
Quick					░░
Crispy	██				
Reheating Leftovers					
Vegetables					

5c

Convection Microwave Utensils

A wide variety of utensils may be used in convection and combination cooking. Many of them are also suitable for microwaving alone. Microwave-only paper and plastic products should not be used for combination cooking or placed in the oven while it is still hot from convection cooking.

Be sure to use hot pads when handling utensils. They become hot from convection and combination cooking.

The Carousel Turntable is a utensil itself: a drip pan under the broiling trivet during roasting and broiling or a baking sheet for breads and cookies.

Baking rack serves as a shelf for two-level cooking, such as layer cakes or cookies. Use it for convection and combination cooking.

Metal and aluminum foil pans are safe for combination as well as convection cooking. During the convection cycle, heat transferred from the pan cooks the bottom and sides of food. During the microwave cycle, energy penetrates from the top.

Oven glass is excellent for convection, combination and microwave cooking. Stoneware and pottery utensils may be used if they are also microwave-safe. See the dish test on page 7. Bagged microwave popcorn must be placed on an overturned glass pie plate placed on the turntable.

Glass ceramic (Pyroceram®) casseroles go from oven to table. They are microwave-safe and resist the heat of surface elements as well as ovens.

Ovenable paper is designed for use in both microwave and conventional ovens up to 400°F., so it's suitable for convection or combination cooking, too. Other paper products used for microwaving alone, such as paper napkins and towels, cannot be used with convection heat.

Thermoset® plastics are heat-resistant to temperatures of 425°F. as well as microwave-safe. They are sold as dual-purpose utensils and can be used. Do not use any other plastics for combination and convection cooking.

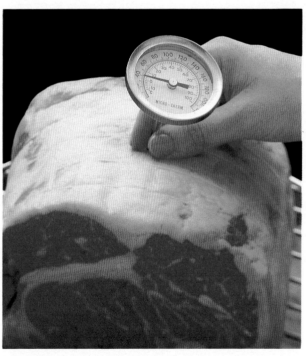

Dual safe microwave/conventional thermometers may be used in the oven during combination cooking. Other thermometers should only be used outside the oven, since microwave thermometers are not heat-resistant and conventional types are not microwave-safe.

CONVECTION MICROWAVE
MAIN DISHES

Stuffed Pork Chops, page 19c

Roasting Techniques

Preheating the oven is not necessary for roasted meat and poultry. Place foods on broiling trivet which holds meat out of its juices. You don't even need a pan because the turntable will catch the drippings. For moist, tender, perfectly done meat in a fraction of the conventional time, just season meat and place it in the oven and cook, following the temperature and time in chart on page 11c.

Optional utensils are metal or foil roasting pans, oven-glass baking dishes or Pyroceram® casseroles. Elevate meat on a heat-resistant rack, if desired, and place utensil on turntable.

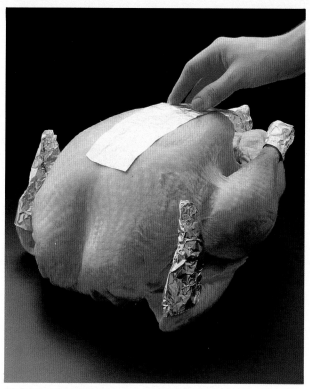

Shield thin or bony areas of roasts or breast, wing tips and legs of birds to prevent overbrowning. Be sure foil does not touch trivet or oven walls.

Roast meat in oven-glass baking dish or shallow Pyroceram® casserole when you wish to make gravy. When meat is done, let it stand on carving board. Microwave gravy in the same dish.

Roast less-tender cuts of beef in heat-resistant and microwave oven-safe covered casserole or in oven cooking bag set in baking dish. Covering helps tenderize meat. You may also use the SLOW COOK setting.

Check doneness after minimum time using a meat thermometer. Removal temperatures are listed on page 11c. If meat is not done, cook 5 minutes longer and check again. Let stand, tented with foil, 5 to 10 minutes before carving.

Dual safe microwave/convection meat thermometer may be inserted in fresh meat before cooking. Other thermometers should only be used outside the oven.

Combination Roasting Chart

Cut		Time	Removal Temperature	Internal Temp. After Standing
Beef				
Roasts (tender cuts)	Rare:	12-14 min. per lb. at HIGH MIX	120°F.	140°F.
	Medium:	13-15 min. per lb. at HIGH MIX	130°F.	150°F.
	Well Done:	14-17 min. per lb. at HIGH MIX	150°F.	160°F.
Roasts (less tender cuts)	Rare:	12-15 min. per lb. at HIGH MIX	120°F.	140°F.
	Medium:	13-17 min. per lb. at HIGH MIX	130°F.	150°F.
	Well Done:	14-18 min. per lb. at HIGH MIX	150°F.	160°F.
Veal				
Roasts (boned, rolled, tied)	Well Done:	14-16 min. per lb. at HIGH MIX	155°F.	165°-170°F.
Breast (stuffed)	Well Done:	11-13 min. per lb. at HIGH MIX	160°F.	170°F.
Pork				
Roasts (boned, rolled, tied or bone-in)	Well Done:	14-16 min. per lb. at HIGH MIX	165°F.	170°F.
Smoked Ham		7-9 min. per lb. at HIGH MIX	130°F.	140°F.
Lamb				
Leg Roasts	Rare:	10-12 min. per lb. at HIGH MIX	120°F.	130°F.
	Medium:	12-14 min. per lb. at HIGH MIX	135°F.	145°F.
	Well Done:	14-16 min. per lb. at HIGH MIX	150°F.	160°F.
Poultry				
Chicken, whole		9-13 min. per lb. at HIGH MIX	175°F.	185°F.
Chicken, pieces		10-12 min. per lb. at *HIGH MIX, 375°F.	175°F.	185°F.
Turkey Breast		13-16 min. per lb. at HIGH MIX	165°F.	170°F.
Turkey (unstuffed)		7-10 min. per lb. at HIGH MIX	175°F.	185°F.

*Necessary to change temperature on HIGH MIX.

Broiling Techniques

Check chart, opposite, for maximum broiling time. Program oven for maximum time, on BROIL or 450°F., following directions in operation manual. Season and slash fat at 1-inch intervals. When audible signal sounds that oven is preheated, quickly put food in oven.

Cook for the minimum time recommended in the chart; then test for doneness. Time varies with the thickness or weight of meat and degree of desired doneness. Turning meat over is not necessary, as moving air cooks it on both sides.

Spray trivet and turntable with nonstick vegetable cooking spray for easy cleanup. Do not cover trivet with aluminum foil, as it blocks the flow of warm air that cooks the food.

Broil food in advance, if desired, then slice. Individual servings may be reheated as needed by microwaving at MEDIUM (50%), following directions on page 19.

Convection Broiling Chart

Cut	Weight/Thickness	Convection Time
Beef		
Rib-eye Steak	¾-1 in. 7-8 oz. each	Rare: 10-13 min. Medium: 14-16 min. Well Done: 17-20 min.
Steaks: Sirloin, Porterhouse, T-bone	1-1½ in.	Rare: 10-13 min. Medium: 14-18 min. Well Done: 19-25 min.
Chuck Steak	1 in.	Rare: 12-14 min. Medium: 15-18 min. Well Done: 19-23 min.
London Broil	1-1¼ in. 2½-3 lbs.	Rare: 23-25 min. Medium: 26-30 min.
Hamburgers	¼ lb. each	Medium: 13-15 min. Well Done: 18-20 min.
Pork		
Chops: loin or center	¾-1 in.	Well Done: 16-20 min.
Bacon	Regular sliced Thick sliced	4-5 min. 7-8 min.
Sausage: Brown 'n Serve	Patties: ½ in., 8 oz. - 1 lb.	8-10 min.
Fresh	Links: 8 oz. - 1 lb.	8-10 min.
Ham slice, fully cooked	¾ in.	10-12 min.
Frankfurters	1 lb.	5-7 min.
Lamb		
Chops: rib, loin or center	¾ in. 3-4 oz. each	Medium: 12-14 min. Well Done 15-17 min.
Chicken		
Broiler-Fryer, halved, quartered or cut up	1-3 lbs.	25-35 min.
Fish		
Fillets	¼-¾ in.	6-7 min.
Steaks	¾ in.	12-14 min.

◄ Pot Roast with Vegetables

4 to 5-pound round or chuck pot roast
½ teaspoon salt
½ teaspoon garlic powder
½ teaspoon dried thyme leaves
⅛ teaspoon pepper
4 potatoes, peeled and quartered
3 onions, quartered
2 carrots, sliced
¾ cup water
2 tablespoons brown bouquet sauce

Makes 8 servings

Place meat in 4-quart casserole. Pat seasonings into meat. Add vegetables. Combine water and browning sauce; pour into casserole dish. Cover.

Roast 20 to 22 minutes per pound on HIGH MIX or until meat is fork-tender. Allow to stand 5 minutes.

Per Serving:			
Calories:	325	Fat:	11 g.
Protein:	36 g.	Cholesterol:	102 mg.
Carbohydrate:	21 g.	Sodium:	227 mg.

Meat Loaf Surprise

1½ pounds ground beef
1 egg
1 small onion, chopped
1 carrot, grated
1 stalk celery, finely chopped
½ cup seasoned bread crumbs
¼ cup catsup
½ teaspoon dried thyme leaves
¼ teaspoon garlic powder
⅛ teaspoon pepper
¼ pound boiled ham, sliced
¼ pound Swiss cheese, sliced

Makes 6 servings

Thoroughly combine all ingredients except ham and cheese. On a sheet of wax paper, press mixture into a 9 × 12-inch rectangle.

Layer sliced ham on meat, then cheese. Roll up, starting at narrow end. Seal ends to form loaf. Place seam side down in loaf pan, 9 × 5 inches. Roast 30 to 35 minutes on HIGH MIX or until internal temperature reaches 155°F. Cover and allow to stand 5 to 10 minutes.

Per Serving:			
Calories:	384	Fat:	23 g.
Protein:	30 g.	Cholesterol:	145 mg.
Carbohydrate:	12 g.	Sodium:	525 mg.

Steak Roulade ▲

¼ cup red wine
¼ cup soy sauce
¼ cup vegetable oil
1½ pounds flank steak
1 medium onion, diced
1 stalk celery, diced
½ green pepper, diced
½ cup sliced mushrooms
2 tablespoons margarine or butter
½ cup seasoned bread crumbs

Makes 4 servings

Combine wine, soy sauce and oil in large dish. Add steak and marinate several hours.

Combine remaining ingredients, except bread crumbs, in small bowl. Microwave at HIGH (100%) until vegetables are tender, 4 to 5 minutes. Stir in crumbs.

Remove meat from marinade. Spread filling evenly over meat. Roll meat up, starting at narrow end. Tie securely with string. Place in glass pie plate and on broiling trivet. Roast 30 minutes on HIGH MIX or until internal temperature reaches 130°F.

Per Serving:			
Calories:	461	Fat:	29 g.
Protein:	35 g.	Cholesterol:	90 mg.
Carbohydrate:	13 g.	Sodium:	536 mg.

Oriental Flank Steak

¼ cup sherry
2 tablespoons packed brown sugar
¾ teaspoon salt
3 tablespoons soy sauce
3 tablespoons Hoisin sauce
3 tablespoons catsup
1 tablespoon minced fresh ginger
2 green onions, thinly sliced
1 to 1½-pound flank steak

Makes 4 servings

Combine all ingredients except flank steak in medium bowl. Pour over steak. Marinate at least 2 hours or overnight. Preheat oven for broiling.

Place flank steak on broiling trivet. Broil in preheated oven 18 to 22 minutes for rare, 22 to 26 minutes for medium, brushing with marinade several times.

Per Serving:			
Calories:	226	Fat:	13 g.
Protein:	22 g.	Cholesterol:	60 mg.
Carbohydrate:	4 g.	Sodium:	421 mg.

◄ Hearty Pizza

1 pound ground beef or
   4 to 6 ounces sliced pepperoni
2 medium onions, chopped
2 cloves garlic, finely chopped
2 tablespoons olive oil
1 can (28 oz.) crushed tomatoes in puree
1 tablespoon dried oregano leaves
1 teaspoon dried basil leaves
½ teaspoon salt
⅛ teaspoon pepper
3 cups all-purpose flour
1 package active dry yeast
½ teaspoon salt
¾ cup milk
¼ cup water
2 tablespoons vegetable oil
2 cups shredded mozzarella cheese (about
   8 ounces)
   Yellow cornmeal

Makes two 12-inch pizzas,
16 servings

If using ground beef, place in a medium-sized bowl. Microwave at HIGH (100%) until beef loses pink color, 4 to 6 minutes, stirring to break up beef after half the cooking time. Drain and set aside.

Combine onion, garlic and olive oil in medium bowl. Microwave at HIGH (100%) until vegetables are tender, 4 to 6 minutes. Stir in crushed tomatoes in puree, spices, ½ teaspoon salt and the pepper.

Microwave at HIGH (100%) until bubbly, about 3 minutes. Stir. Reduce power to MEDIUM (50%). Microwave until thickened, 6 to 8 minutes.

Mix flour, yeast and ½ teaspoon salt in large bowl. Stir in milk, water and oil to make a pliable dough. Knead until smooth, about 2 minutes. Place in well-greased large bowl; turn greased side up. Cover with clean, moist towel. Place in oven at 100°F. until double in size, about 40 minutes. (Dough is ready if an indentation remains when touched.)

Remove dough and turntable from oven. Preheat oven to 425°F. Punch down dough. Divide dough in half. With well-greased fingers, pat dough onto 2 greased 12 × ⅝-inch metal pizza pans, which have been sprinkled with cornmeal. Pinch dough to form edge. Prick crust. Bake on turntable and baking rack 12 to 15 minutes or until crusts are golden brown. Top crusts with pizza sauce, ground beef or pepperoni and cheese. Bake at 425°F., 6 to 10 minutes or until cheese is melted and beginning to brown.

Per Serving:			
Calories:	245	Fat:	11 g.
Protein:	12 g.	Cholesterol:	26 mg.
Carbohydrate:	24 g.	Sodium:	333 mg.

Tamale Casserole

1 pound lean ground beef
1 medium onion, chopped
1 small green pepper, chopped
2 cans (8 ounces each) tomato sauce
1 clove garlic, minced
1 teaspoon chili powder
1 teaspoon taco seasoning mix
½ teaspoon sugar
¼ teaspoon salt
¼ teaspoon pepper

Corn Bread:
½ cup yellow cornmeal
½ cup all-purpose flour
2 teaspoons baking powder
1 tablespoon sugar
¼ teaspoon salt
½ cup milk
1 egg
2 tablespoons melted shortening

Topping:
½ cup shredded Cheddar cheese (about
   2 ounces)
¼ cup sliced pitted black olives

Makes 6 servings

Mix ground beef, onion and green pepper in 2-quart casserole. Microwave at HIGH (100%) 5 minutes, stirring to break up beef after half the cooking time. Stir in tomato sauce, garlic, chili powder, taco seasoning mix, sugar, salt and pepper. Microwave at HIGH (100%) 5 minutes. Reduce power to MEDIUM-HIGH (70%). Microwave 5 minutes.

Combine cornmeal, flour, baking powder, sugar and salt in medium bowl. Stir in milk, egg and shortening. Beat mixture until almost smooth.

Pour over beef mixture. Bake 25 minutes on *HIGH MIX, 375°F. or until corn bread is golden. Sprinkle with topping ingredients. Cool 5 minutes before serving.

*Necessary to change temperature on HIGH MIX.

Per Serving:			
Calories:	341	Fat:	16 g.
Protein:	22 g.	Cholesterol:	108 mg.
Carbohydrate:	27 g.	Sodium:	909 mg.

Ginger Pork Kabobs

1 egg, beaten
½ cup crushed chow mein noodles
¼ cup apple juice
2 tablespoons soy sauce
1 tablespoon grated gingerroot
1 pound ground pork
1 can (8 ounces) pineapple chunks (juice pack), drained
1 large red pepper, cut into ¾-inch chunks
½ cup apple juice
2 tablespoons cider vinegar
1 teaspoon cornstarch

Makes 4 servings

Mix egg, crushed noodles, ¼ cup apple juice, soy sauce and gingerroot. Crumble ground pork into mixture; blend thoroughly, shape into 1-inch balls. Set aside.

For glaze, mix ½ cup apple juice, vinegar and cornstarch in small bowl. Microwave at HIGH (100%) until thickened, 1½ to 3 minutes, stirring every 30 seconds.

Preheat oven for broiling. Thread pork balls alternately with pineapple and red pepper chunks on 4 wooden or metal skewers. Place on broiling trivet.

Brush kabobs with glaze. Broil in preheated oven 15 to 20 minutes. Brush with remaining glaze before serving.

Per Serving:			
Calories:	256	Fat:	7 g.
Protein:	29 g.	Cholesterol:	153 mg.
Carbohydrate:	18 g.	Sodium:	652 mg.

Steak Kabobs ▲

¼ cup sugar
¼ cup soy sauce
¼ cup white wine
1 tablespoon vegetable oil
1 teaspoon ground ginger
¼ teaspoon salt
2 pounds lean top beef round steak, cut into 1-inch cubes
2 large green peppers, cut into chunks
2 medium tomatoes, cut into quarters
1 can (8 ounces) pineapple chunks (juice pack), drained

Makes 4 servings

Mix sugar, soy sauce, wine, oil, ginger and salt in medium bowl. Stir in steak cubes; cover. Marinate at room temperature 1 hour or at least 4 hours in refrigerator.

Preheat oven for broiling. Remove steak cubes from marinade; reserve marinade. Thread steak cubes alternately with remaining ingredients on 8 wooden or metal skewers. Place on broiling trivet. Broil 7 to 9 minutes or until desired doneness, brushing with marinade after half the time.

Note: Skewers up to 12 inches can be used.

Per Serving:			
Calories:	432	Fat:	17 g.
Protein:	52 g.	Cholesterol:	153 mg.
Carbohydrate:	15 g.	Sodium:	381 mg.

Stuffed Pork Chops

4 pork chops, 1¼ inches thick
1 cup chopped apple
½ cup soft bread crumbs
½ cup chopped walnuts
¼ cup chopped onion
¼ cup raisins
1 egg
1 teaspoon dried parsley flakes
½ teaspoon dried thyme leaves
¼ teaspoon ground sage
⅛ teaspoon pepper

Makes 4 servings

Make pocket in each chop. Combine remaining ingredients; mix well. Stuff each chop with one-fourth of the mixture. Place chops directly on turntable or round baking pan.

Roast 30 minutes on HIGH MIX or until meat next to bone is no longer pink.

Per Serving:			
Calories:	451	Fat:	26 g.
Protein:	36 g.	Cholesterol:	156 mg.
Carbohydrate:	19 g.	Sodium:	100 mg.

Pineapple Pork Roast

1 cup pineapple preserves
¼ cup prepared mustard
1 tablespoon prepared horseradish
1 tablespoon soy sauce
3 to 5-pound pork roast

Makes 6 servings

Combine all ingredients except pork roast in small bowl. Place roast on broiling trivet.

Roast 14 to 16 minutes per pound on HIGH MIX or until internal temperature reaches 165°F.

Cover roast with sauce during last 20 minutes of cooking. Cover and let stand 10 minutes before serving. Extra sauce may be heated and served with roast.

Per Serving:			
Calories:	394	Fat:	15 g.
Protein:	29 g.	Cholesterol:	93 mg.
Carbohydrate:	36 g.	Sodium:	376 mg.

Convert your own casserole recipes.

Bake 25 to 30 minutes on HIGH MIX or until thoroughly heated.

Glazed Stuffed Cornish Hens ▲

1 cup chopped pecans
¾ cup apricot preserves
¼ cup margarine or butter, melted
3 tablespoons orange juice concentrate
1 tablespoon lemon juice
1 cup seasoned stuffing cubes
½ cup water
2 Cornish hens (1½ pounds each)

Makes 4 servings

Combine pecans, preserves, melted margarine, orange juice concentrate and lemon juice. Combine half the sauce mixture with stuffing cubes and water. Stuff cavity of each bird. Truss birds.

Pour half of the remaining sauce over hens. Brush with remaining sauce halfway through cooking time.

Roast 13 to 15 minutes per pound on HIGH MIX or until meat next to bone is no longer pink. Internal temperature of stuffing should register 165°F.

Per Serving:			
Calories:	743	Fat:	36 g.
Protein:	34 g.	Cholesterol:	74 mg.
Carbohydrate:	75 g.	Sodium:	670 mg.

Roast Chicken

1 teaspoon ground ginger
½ teaspoon ground coriander
  Dash of pepper
5 to 6-pound roasting chicken
2 tablespoons margarine or butter
½ cup minced onion
½ cup plain yogurt
½ cup half-and-half
1 teaspoon turmeric
½ teaspoon salt

Makes 6 servings

Combine ginger, coriander and pepper; rub into chicken. Tie legs of chicken; place breast side up on broiling trivet on turntable.

Place margarine in a medium bowl. Microwave at HIGH (100%) until melted, 30 to 45 seconds. Blend in remaining ingredients. Reserve one-fourth cup of the mixture; set aside. Spread remaining mixture over chicken.

Roast 10 to 12 minutes per pound on HIGH MIX or until chicken next to bone is no longer pink. Combine pan drippings and reserved sauce. Microwave at HIGH (100%) until hot, about 1 minute. Serve with chicken.

Per Serving:			
Calories:	284	Fat:	15 g.
Protein:	32 g.	Cholesterol:	100 mg.
Carbohydrate:	4 g.	Sodium:	337 mg.

Mustard and Mayonnaise Chicken

2½ to 3-pound broiler-fryer chicken, cut up
¼ cup spicy prepared mustard
¼ cup mayonnaise

Makes 5 servings

Arrange chicken pieces skin side up on round baking pan or directly on turntable. Combine mustard and mayonnaise; spread on chicken pieces.

Roast 35 minutes on HIGH MIX or until chicken next to bone is no longer pink.

Per Serving:			
Calories:	233	Fat:	15 g.
Protein:	21 g.	Cholesterol:	72 mg.
Carbohydrate:	—	Sodium:	479 mg.

Poultry Pie

Filling:
3 cups diced, cooked boneless chicken or turkey
1 package (10 ounces) frozen peas, defrosted
1 can (10¾ ounces) condensed cream of
  mushroom soup
½ cup milk
2 tablespoons chopped pimiento
½ teaspoon dried oregano leaves
½ teaspoon dried marjoram leaves
½ teaspoon salt
¼ teaspoon dried thyme leaves
¼ teaspoon garlic powder
⅛ teaspoon pepper

Crust:
1 cup all-purpose flour
1¼ teaspoons baking powder
½ teaspoon salt
¼ cup margarine or butter
3 to 5 tablespoons milk

Makes 8 servings

Combine filling ingredients in a 9-inch deep-dish pie pan; set aside.

Combine flour, baking powder and salt in medium bowl. Cut in margarine until mixture resembles coarse crumbs. Add enough milk to form a soft dough. Roll out on lightly floured surface to fit top of dish. Fit dough onto dish. Trim, seal and flute. Cut small slits in crust.

Place on broiling trivet. Bake 25 to 30 minutes on *LOW MIX, 375°F., or until thoroughly heated and top is browned.

*Necessary to change temperature on LOW MIX.

Per Serving:			
Calories:	284	Fat:	13 g.
Protein:	20 g.	Cholesterol:	49 mg.
Carbohydrate:	21 g.	Sodium:	774 mg.

Broiled Chicken

1 cup dry white wine
1 medium onion, chopped
1 tablespoon dried thyme leaves
½ teaspoon salt
½ teaspoon garlic powder
⅛ teaspoon pepper
2½ to 3-pound broiler-fryer chicken, cut up

Makes 4 servings

Combine all ingredients except chicken. Place chicken skin side down in large dish. Pour marinade over chicken. Marinate 2 hours.

Preheat oven for broiling. Remove chicken from marinade; reserve marinade. Place chicken pieces on broiling trivet. Broil until chicken next to bone is no longer pink, about 30 minutes.

Pour marinade into small bowl. Microwave at HIGH (100%) until onion is soft, about 2 minutes. Pour over chicken pieces.

Per Serving:			
Calories:	235	Fat:	7 g.
Protein:	27 g.	Cholesterol:	81 mg.
Carbohydrate:	5 g.	Sodium:	349 mg.

Stuffed Turkey Loaf

1 package (6 ounces) stuffing mix
1½ pounds ground turkey or ground beef
1 egg, slightly beaten
1 small onion, finely chopped
½ cup quick-cooking oats
½ cup applesauce
½ teaspoon salt
⅛ teaspoon white pepper
¼ teaspoon ground thyme
½ teaspoon poultry seasoning
1 teaspoon Worcestershire sauce
Turkey gravy (1 can, jar or prepared dry mix)

Makes 6 servings

Per Serving:			
Calories:	369	Fat:	17 g.
Protein:	25 g.	Cholesterol:	106 mg.
Carbohydrate:	30 g.	Sodium:	964 mg.

Herb Roasted Chicken

3 tablespoons margarine or butter, softened
1 clove garlic, minced
3 tablespoons grated Parmesan cheese
½ teaspoon ground sage
¾ teaspoon thyme leaves
¾ teaspoon basil leaves
5 to 6 pound roasting chicken

Makes 6 servings

Cream together margarine, garlic, Parmesan cheese, sage, thyme and basil.

Turn chicken breast side up and work your fingers under the skin at the openings on each side of the breast. Continue into thigh and leg and make the skin as smooth as possible. Using fingers, spread herb mixture evenly under skin.

Place chicken, breast side up on broiling trivet. Bake 9 to 13 minutes per pound on HIGH MIX or until chicken next to bone is no longer pink.

Per Serving:			
Calories:	270	Fat:	15 g.
Protein:	32 g.	Cholesterol:	94 mg.
Carbohydrate:	1 g.	Sodium:	216 mg.

Prepare stuffing according to package directions for microwaving. Set aside 2 cups. Place remaining stuffing in small casserole to be reheated later.

Thoroughly combine remaining ingredients, except for turkey gravy. In a 10-inch glass pie plate, shape ½ of the mixture into an oval. Flatten center being sure to leave one-inch sides.

Place reserved 2 cups of stuffing inside the center. Cover with remaining meat mixture. Press to seal edges and form a loaf shape. Roast 30 to 35 minutes on HIGH MIX or until internal temperature in center of stuffing reaches 170°F. Let stand, covered, 10 minutes before slicing. Slice and serve with heated gravy and reheated leftover stuffing.

Sesame Oven-Fried Chicken ▲

  1 egg
  ½ cup milk
  ½ cup all-purpose flour
  2 tablespoons sesame seed
  1 teaspoon baking powder
  2 teaspoons paprika
  1 teaspoon garlic powder
  ½ teaspoon salt
  2½ to 3½-pound broiler-fryer chicken, cut up
  ½ cup margarine or butter, melted

Makes 5 servings

Beat egg and milk in medium bowl. Combine flour, sesame seed, baking powder, paprika, garlic powder and salt in plastic or paper bag. Dip chicken pieces in egg mixture, then shake in bag to coat. Arrange chicken pieces skin side up on turntable. Pour margarine evenly over chicken. Bake 35 minutes on *HIGH MIX, 375°F.

*Necessary to change temperature on HIGH MIX.

Per Serving:			
Calories:	399	Fat:	27 g.
Protein:	26 g.	Cholesterol:	122 mg.
Carbohydrate:	12 g.	Sodium:	578 mg.

Honey Mustard Chicken

  ½ cup coarse ground mustard
  ¼ cup Dijon-style mustard
  ¼ cup honey
  2 to 3 pounds boneless chicken breasts and thighs, skin removed

Makes 4 servings

Combine coarse mustard, Dijon mustard and honey. Set aside.

Preheat oven for broiling. Place chicken in 9-inch oven-safe dish. Put dish on broiling trivet and broil in pre-heated oven 25 to 30 minutes or until chicken is no longer pink. When chicken is about half cooked, pour off any liquid and brush with sauce to cover chicken pieces completely.

Per Serving:			
Calories:	368	Fat:	8 g.
Protein:	50 g.	Cholesterol:	133 mg.
Carbohydrate:	19 g.	Sodium:	950 mg.

◀ Broiled Salmon with Basil Sauce

2 tablespoons olive oil
1 clove garlic, minced
¼ cup white wine
2 tablespoons lemon juice
1 cup fresh basil*
¼ cup grated Parmesan cheese
½ teaspoon Dijon-style mustard
4 salmon steaks (1¼ to 1½ pounds) or haddock, halibut, swordfish
  Cayenne pepper

Makes 4 servings

Combine oil, garlic, white wine and lemon juice in blender. Add basil, Parmesan cheese and mustard and blend until smooth. Preheat oven for broiling.

Put one-fourth of basil sauce in bottom of 9-inch oven-safe dish. Arrange steaks on sauce and pour remaining sauce over tops of steaks. Sprinkle with cayenne.

Place dish on broiling trivet and broil in preheated oven 20 to 24 minutes or until fish flakes easily when tested with a fork.

*If not available substitute ½ cup fresh parsley and 2 tablespoons dried basil.

Per Serving:			
Calories:	357	Fat:	21 g.
Protein:	35 g.	Cholesterol:	97 mg.
Carbohydrate:	2 g.	Sodium:	209 mg.

Crunchy Crab Boats

1 can (6 ounces) fancy white crabmeat, drained
1 package (3 ounces) cream cheese, softened
½ cup chopped almonds
2 tablespoons green onions, chopped
1 tablespoon dry white wine
1 teaspoon lemon juice
1 teaspoon prepared horseradish
¼ teaspoon garlic powder
¼ teaspoon salt
  Dash of white pepper
  Dash of cayenne pepper
2 hard rolls, cut in half
¼ cup shredded Swiss cheese

Makes 4 servings

Spicy Shrimp

¼ cup white wine
¼ cup water
3 tablespoons soy sauce
2 tablespoons sugar
1 tablespoon vegetable oil
2 teaspoons dried parsley flakes
⅛ to ¼ teaspoon ground ginger
  Dash of hot pepper sauce
1 pound jumbo raw shrimp, shelled and deveined

Makes 4 servings

Mix all ingredients except shrimp in medium bowl. Stir in shrimp; cover. Marinate at room temperature 45 minutes or 3 hours in refrigerator.

Preheat oven for broiling. Remove shrimp from marinade; reserve marinade. Place shrimp on round baking pan. Broil 6 to 8 minutes, brushing with marinade after half the time.

Microwave remaining marinade at HIGH (100%) 2 minutes. Serve over rice or as a dipping sauce when served as an appetizer, if desired.

Per Serving:			
Calories:	109	Fat:	2 g.
Protein:	18 g.	Cholesterol:	129 mg.
Carbohydrate:	3 g.	Sodium:	319 mg.

Preheat oven for broiling. Remove any bits of shell or cartilage from crab. Combine with next 10 ingredients. Mix well. Set aside.

Spread one-fourth of crab filling on each roll half. Place Swiss cheese on top of each. Place on broiling trivet.

Broil in preheated oven 8 to 10 minutes or until cheese is melted and crab is hot. Sprinkle with paprika and serve.

Per Serving:			
Calories:	292	Fat:	19 g.
Protein:	15 g.	Cholesterol:	57 mg.
Carbohydrate:	15 g.	Sodium:	416 mg.

Cheese Soufflé ▲

¼ cup margarine or butter
¼ cup all-purpose flour
½ teaspoon salt
⅛ teaspoon cayenne pepper
1½ cups milk
2 cups shredded Cheddar cheese (about 8 ounces)
6 eggs, separated

Makes 4 servings

Place margarine in large bowl. Microwave at HIGH (100%) until melted, about 1 minute. Blend in flour, salt and cayenne. Gradually stir in milk. Microwave at MEDIUM-HIGH (70%) until slightly thickened, about 6 minutes, stirring every 2 minutes. Add cheese. Microwave at MEDIUM-HIGH (70%) 2 minutes; stir to blend.

Preheat oven to 325°F. Beat egg yolks. Stir a small amount of hot sauce gradually into egg yolks; return to sauce, blending well. Cool slightly.

Beat egg whites until soft peaks form. With rubber spatula fold egg whites into cheese sauce, half at a time, just until blended. Pour into greased 2-quart soufflé dish. Bake 30 to 35 minutes on *LOW MIX, 325°F. or until top is puffed and golden and center is set. Serve immediately.

*Necessary to change temperature on LOW MIX.

Per Serving:			
Calories:	531	Fat:	41 g.
Protein:	27 g.	Cholesterol:	478 mg.
Carbohydrate:	12 g.	Sodium:	912 mg.

Frittata ▲

¾ cup diced green pepper
¾ cup diced mushrooms
¾ cup diced zucchini
¾ cup diced onion
½ cup diced pimiento
2 tablespoons vegetable oil
6 eggs
2 packages (8 ounces each) cream cheese
¼ cup milk
2 cups cubed bread (3 slices)
1½ cups shredded Cheddar cheese
1 teaspoon salt
½ teaspoon garlic powder
¼ teaspoon pepper

Makes 8 servings

Combine vegetables and oil in medium bowl; cover. Microwave at HIGH (100%) until vegetables are tender, about 5 minutes. Drain liquid.

Beat eggs with cream cheese and milk until smooth. Mix in remaining ingredients. Pour into buttered 9-inch spring form pan.

Bake 30 minutes on LOW MIX or until set in center. Cool 10 to 20 minutes. Cut into wedges.

Per Serving:			
Calories:	426	Fat:	36 g.
Protein:	16 g.	Cholesterol:	292 mg.
Carbohydrate:	12 g.	Sodium:	685 mg.

Strawberry Puff Ring, page 41c

Convection-Only Techniques

Preheating the oven is necessary with convection cooking of smaller, faster-cooking food items that require less than 20 minutes of baking. Foods requiring longer baking time use LOW MIX.

Two-level baking allows baking of two pans of cookies, small muffins or pizzas at the same time. Round baking pans are excellent cooking utensils for many convection-only items.

Convenience foods such as frozen appetizers, pizzas, egg rolls and refrigerated bread products bake and brown quickly with convection-only cooking. Follow package directions for conventional baking times.

Cake Techniques

Layer Cakes. Use a mix or your own conventional recipe. Follow recipe or package directions for preheating and baking instructions. Use baking rack and turntable to bake two layers at once.

Tube or Bundt Cakes. Do not preheat oven. Bake cakes for three-fourths of time on recipe or package directions using LOW MIX. Bake cake on broiling trivet. If arcing occurs with fluted tube pan, place a heat-and-microwave-safe dish or plate between pan and broiling trivet.

Angel Food. Do not preheat oven. Bake your recipe or a mix 25 to 30 minutes on LOW MIX or until crust is golden brown, firm and looks very dry.

Loaf Cakes or Quick Breads. Do not preheat oven. Bake for three-fourths of time on recipe or package directions using LOW MIX. Test for doneness at minimum time. If loaf is not done, let stand in oven a few minutes to complete cooking.

Pie Techniques

Pie Shell. Use mix, frozen pie dough, or your recipe for single crust pie. Prick crust with fork. Preheat oven to 425°F. Place pie shell on broiling trivet; bake with convection heat 8 to 10 minutes or until lightly browned. Cool and fill.

Double Crust or Crumb Top Pies. Prepare pie as you would for conventional baking; make slits in top of two crust pie. Preheat oven to 400°F. Place pie on broiling trivet. Bake double crust or lattice pies 25 to 35 minutes on *HIGH MIX, 400°F.; crumb top pies 20 to 25 minutes on *HIGH MIX, 400°F. (*Necessary to change temperature on HIGH MIX).

Custard Pies. Prebake and cool pie shell as directed above. Fill with uncooked custard. Without preheating, bake pie on round baking pan placed on broiling trivet for 30 to 35 minutes on *LOW MIX, 325°F. If custard is not set, let stand in oven a few minutes to complete cooking. (*Necessary to change temperature on LOW MIX).

Frozen Prepared Custard-Type Pies. Preheat oven to temperature listed on package. Place pie on broiling trivet. Bake three-fourths of package time using LOW MIX set at the package temperature. If filling is not set, let stand in oven to complete cooking. **Frozen Prepared Fruit Pies.** Do not preheat oven. Bake on broiling trivet. Use *HIGH MIX, 375°F. Bake 8-inch, 35 minutes; 9-inch, 40 to 45 minutes. (*Necessary to change temperature on HIGH MIX).

Bread & Baking Techniques

Proofing dough. Use your own recipe or frozen dough. Place in well-greased bowl or loaf pan; cover with damp cloth. Place in oven at *SLOW COOK 100°F. 30 to 45 minutes. Frozen dough will take longer, 2 to 2¾ hours. Dough is doubled when impressions remain after fingers are pressed ½ inch into dough. (*Necessary to change temperature on SLOW COOK.)

Preheating of oven is not necessary. Bake one loaf 25 minutes and two loaves 30 minutes at LOW MIX. After baking, bread should be golden brown and sound hollow when tapped. Do not let bread stand in oven; remove from pans immediately to cool on wire rack.

Braid or other shape. Remove turntable from oven. Shape bread; place directly on turntable. No preheating is needed. Bake for three-fourths of the time in your conventional recipe on LOW MIX.

Combination Baking Chart

Item	Procedure
Cakes: Your recipe or mix	
Tube or Bundt Cakes**	Bake on broiling trivet three-fourths the recommended time on LOW MIX.
Angel Food	Bake 25 to 30 minutes on LOW MIX.
Loaf Cakes or Quick Breads	Bake three-fourths the recommended time on LOW MIX.
Bar Cookies: Your recipe or mix	Bake three-fourths the recommended time or until wooden pick inserted in center comes out clean on LOW MIX.
Pies	
Single Crust: baked before filling, your recipe, mix or frozen prepared	Prick crust with fork. Preheat oven to 425°F. Bake on broiling trivet 8 to 10 minutes or until lightly browned. Let cool before filling.
Double Crust	Preheat oven to 400°F. Bake on broiling trivet 25 to 35 minutes on *HIGH MIX 400°F.
Crumb Top	Preheat oven to 400°F. Bake on broiling trivet 20 to 25 minutes on *HIGH MIX 400°F.
Custard Pie	Prebake, following directions for single crust; cool. Fill with desired uncooked custard. Bake on round baking pan on broiling trivet 35 minutes on *LOW MIX 325°F. If custard is not set, let stand in oven a few minutes.
Pecan Pie	Preheat oven to 350°F. Bake on broiling trivet 25 to 30 minutes on LOW MIX.
Frozen Prepared Fruit Pies	Place on broiling trivet and bake 30 to 40 minutes using *HIGH MIX 375°F.
Frozen Prepared Custard Pies	Preheat oven to package temperature. Place on broiling trivet and bake three-fourths of package time using LOW MIX and package temperature. If not set, let stand in oven a few minutes.
Breads	
Loaf: Your recipe or frozen, defrosted and proofed	Bake 25 to 30 minutes on LOW MIX for 1 to 2 loaves.
Braid or other shape	Remove metal turntable from oven. Place bread directly on metal turntable. Bake on LOW MIX for three-fourths the conventional time.
Muffins	
Large, bakery-style	Bake three-fourths the recommended package or recipe time on LOW MIX.
Desserts	
Cheesecake	Bake three-fourths the recipe time on LOW MIX or until center is nearly set.
Crisps and Cobblers	Bake three-fourths the recipe time on LOW MIX.

**If arcing occurs while using a fluted tube pan, place a heat-resistant dish (Pyrex® pie plate, glass pizza tray or dinner plate) between the pan and the broiling trivet.

*Necessary to change temperature on HIGH MIX and LOW MIX.

Convection Baking Chart

Item (for foods requiring 25 minutes or less)	Baking Time and Temperature
Appetizers: Brown and serve, pastry	Follow package directions.
Biscuits: Your recipe, mix or refrigerator	Follow recipe or package directions.
Cookies: Drop, rolled, refrigerator, spritz, molded	Follow recipe or package directions.
Fish Sticks: Frozen	Follow package directions.
Layer Cakes: Your recipe or mix	Follow recipe or package directions.
Muffins: Your recipe or mix	Follow recipe or package directions.
Pizza: Your recipe or frozen	Follow recipe or package directions.
Puff Pastry: Your recipe or frozen	Follow recipe or package directions.
Rolls: Your recipe, package or refrigerator	Follow recipe or package directions.

◄ Chocolate Chip Bars

2¼ cups all-purpose flour
 1 teaspoon baking soda
 ½ teaspoon salt
 ¾ cup granulated sugar
 ¾ cup packed brown sugar
 ½ cup margarine or butter
 ½ cup vegetable oil
 1 teaspoon vanilla
 2 eggs
 1 package (12 ounces) chocolate chips
 1 cup chopped nuts

Makes 32 bars

Combine flour, soda and salt; set aside. Cream together sugars, margarine, oil and vanilla. Beat until creamy. Beat in eggs. Gradually add flour mixture; mix well. Stir in chocolate chips and nuts.

Spread mixture into 2 ungreased square pans, 8 × 8 inches. Bake 20 to 25 minutes on LOW MIX or until wooden pick inserted in center comes out clean. Let cool in pans. Cut into 32 squares.

Per Serving:			
Calories:	208	Fat:	13 g.
Protein:	2 g.	Cholesterol:	17 mg.
Carbohydrate:	23 g.	Sodium:	108 mg.

◄ Peanut Butter Cookies

 ½ cup peanut butter
 ½ cup granulated sugar
 ½ cup packed brown sugar
 ¼ cup margarine or butter
 ¼ cup vegetable shortening
 1 egg
1¼ cups all-purpose flour
 ¾ teaspoon baking soda
 ½ teaspoon baking powder

Makes 3 dozen

Combine peanut butter, sugars, margarine, shortening and egg; beat until smooth. Blend in flour, baking soda and baking powder. Preheat oven to 375°F.

Shape dough into ¾-inch balls. Place 2 inches apart on lightly greased round baking pans. With fork, flatten in crisscross pattern.

Bake 12 minutes at 375°F. or until set but not hard. Cool on wire racks.

Per Serving:			
Calories:	85	Fat:	5 g.
Protein:	2 g.	Cholesterol:	8 mg.
Carbohydrate:	10 g.	Sodium:	62 mg.

Autumn Treasure Cookies

1 cup all-purpose flour
¼ teaspoon salt
¼ teaspoon baking powder
¼ teaspoon baking soda
½ cup packed brown sugar
½ cup granulated sugar
½ cup butter-flavor shortening
1 egg
1 cup rolled oats
1 teaspoon vanilla
½ cup Reese's Pieces® candy
½ cup M & M® candies (only orange, yellow and browns)

Makes 32 cookies

Preheat oven to 350°F. Grease 2 round baking pans; set aside.

Sift first 4 ingredients. Blend sugars and shortening. Add egg and beat well. Add the sifted mixture and mix well.

Add oats, vanilla and candies. Blend together well.

Drop by rounded tablespoonfuls onto prepared sheets. Bake 12 to 15 minutes at 350°F. or until golden brown. Cool cookies on wire racks.

Per Serving:			
Calories:	112	Fat:	5 g.
Protein:	2 g.	Cholesterol:	9 mg.
Carbohydrate:	15 g.	Sodium:	36 mg.

Orange Oatmeal Chippers

½ cup margarine or butter, softened
⅓ cup oil
¾ cup packed brown sugar
¼ cup granulated sugar
2 eggs
1 teaspoon orange extract
2 cups quick-cooking rolled oats
1 cup all-purpose flour
½ cup whole wheat flour
1 teaspoon baking soda
½ teaspoon salt
1 cup raisins or chocolate chips
1 tablespoon grated orange peel
½ cup coarsely chopped nuts

Makes 4 dozen

Carousel Crackles

1 cup semisweet chocolate chips
1 cup packed brown sugar
⅓ cup vegetable oil
2 eggs
1 teaspoon vanilla
1 cup all-purpose flour
1 teaspoon baking powder
¼ teaspoon salt
½ cup finely chopped walnuts
½ cup powdered sugar

Makes 4 dozen

Place chocolate chips in large mixing bowl. Microwave at HIGH (100%) until melted, about 2 minutes. Blend in brown sugar and oil. Add eggs, 1 at a time, beating well after each. Stir in vanilla. Combine flour, baking powder and salt; stir into chocolate mixture. Mix in nuts. Chill dough at least 1 hour.

Preheat oven to 350°F. Drop dough by rounded teaspoonfuls into powdered sugar; roll to coat. Place 2 inches apart on greased turntable or round baking pans. Bake 10 to 12 minutes at 350°F. Cool on wire racks.

Per Serving:			
Calories:	72	Fat:	4 g.
Protein:	1 g.	Cholesterol:	6 mg.
Carbohydrate:	10 g.	Sodium:	20 mg.

Preheat oven to 350°F. Cream together margarine, oil and sugars. Beat until creamy. Beat in eggs and orange extract; blend well.

Add rolled oats, flours, baking soda and salt; mix well. Stir in raisins or chocolate chips, orange peel and nuts.

Drop dough by teaspoonfuls 2 inches apart on greased round baking pans. Bake 8 to 12 minutes at 350°F. or until light golden brown. Cool on wire racks.

Per Serving:			
Calories:	95	Fat:	5 g.
Protein:	2 g.	Cholesterol:	11 mg.
Carbohydrate:	12 g.	Sodium:	72 mg.

◄ Chocolate Meringue Pie

¾ cup sugar
2 tablespoons cornstarch
2 cups milk
2 squares (1 ounce each) unsweetened chocolate
3 eggs, separated
2 tablespoons margarine or butter
1 teaspoon grated orange peel
1 9-inch baked pie shell
½ teaspoon cream of tartar
6 tablespoons sugar

Makes 8 servings

Mix sugar and cornstarch in medium bowl. Stir in milk. Add chocolate squares. Microwave at HIGH (100%) until smooth and thick, 6 to 8 minutes, stirring after 3 minutes. Stir a small amount of chocolate mixture into egg yolks; return to hot chocolate mixture, blending well. Microwave at MEDIUM-HIGH (70%) 3 minutes, stirring once. Stir in margarine and orange peel until margarine is melted. Pour into pie shell. Set aside.

Preheat oven to 425°F. Beat egg whites and cream of tartar until foamy. Beat in sugar, 1 tablespoon at a time; continue beating until stiff and glossy. Spoon meringue onto chocolate filling; spread over filling, carefully sealing meringue to edge of crust. Bake 8 to 10 minutes at 425°F. or until meringue is brown.

Per Serving:			
Calories:	349	Fat:	17 g.
Protein:	6 g.	Cholesterol:	108 mg.
Carbohydrate:	45 g.	Sodium:	228 mg.

Cheesecake ▲

Crust:
1¼ cups all-purpose flour
¾ cup margarine or butter
¼ cup sugar
1 egg yolk
Grated lemon peel from ½ lemon

Filling:
4 packages (8 ounces each) cream cheese
1¼ cups sugar
2 tablespoons all-purpose flour
4 eggs
1 egg yolk
2 tablespoons heavy cream
Grated lemon peel from ½ lemon

Makes 12 servings

Combine crust ingredients in small bowl; beat until well mixed. Refrigerate, covered, 1 hour.

Preheat oven to 400°F. Press one-third flour mixture into bottom of 9-inch spring form pan. Bake at 400°F. 8 minutes; cool.

In large bowl, beat cream cheese until smooth. Slowly beat in sugar. Add flour and remaining ingredients. Beat 5 minutes. Press remaining dough around side of pan to within 1 inch of top; do not bake. Pour cream cheese mixture into pan.

Bake 35 minutes on LOW MIX or until set. Let cheesecake remain in oven 30 minutes. Remove; cool in pan.

Per Serving:			
Calories:	560	Fat:	42 g.
Protein:	10 g.	Cholesterol:	223 mg.
Carbohydrate:	38 g.	Sodium:	383 mg.

Harvest Fruit Pie ▲

- 2 cups all-purpose flour
- 1 teaspoon salt
- 1 teaspoon ground cinnamon
- ⅔ cup plus 2 tablespoons vegetable shortening
- 4 to 5 tablespoons cold water
- ¾ cup sugar
- ¼ cup all-purpose flour
- ½ teaspoon ground cinnamon
- ½ teaspoon ground nutmeg
- 6 cups sliced, peeled apples and pears
- 2 tablespoons margarine or butter
- 1 tablespoon milk
- 1 tablespoon sugar

Makes 8 servings

Preheat oven to 400°F. Combine 2 cups flour, the salt and 1 teaspoon cinnamon in medium bowl. Cut in shortening. Sprinkle in water, 1 tablespoon at a time, until flour is moistened. Gather dough into ball; divide in half. Roll each half into 9-inch circle. Ease 1 circle into 9-inch pie pan.

Combine ¾ cup sugar, ¼ cup flour, ½ teaspoon cinnamon and the nutmeg; mix with apples and pears. Turn into pastry-lined pan; dot with margarine. Cover with top crust. Brush crust with milk; sprinkle with 1 tablespoon sugar. Trim, seal and flute. Cut small slits in top crust.

Place on broiling trivet. Bake 35 minutes on *HIGH MIX, 400°F. or until juices begin to bubble.

*Necessary to change temperature on HIGH MIX.

Per Serving:			
Calories:	469	Fat:	23 g.
Protein:	4 g.	Cholesterol:	—
Carbohydrate:	63 g.	Sodium:	302 mg.

Peach Küchen

- 1 cup all-purpose flour
- 1 tablespoon sugar
- ¼ teaspoon salt
- ¼ teaspoon baking powder
- ¼ cup margarine or butter
- 4 to 5 medium peaches, peeled and sliced or 1 package (20 ounces) frozen peaches, defrosted and drained
- ¼ cup sugar
- 1 teaspoon ground cinnamon
- 1 cup dairy sour cream
- 1 egg yolk, slightly beaten
- 1 teaspoon vanilla

Makes 8 servings

Combine flour, 1 tablespoon sugar, salt and baking powder in medium bowl; mix well. Using a pastry blender, cut in margarine until mixture resembles coarse crumbs. Turn mixture into baking pan, 8 × 8 inches. Pat evenly over bottom and one-fourth way up the sides.

Arrange peaches on top of flour mixture. Combine sugar and cinnamon; sprinkle over peaches. Combine sour cream, egg yolk and vanilla; pour over peach mixture.

Bake 30 minutes on *LOW MIX, 375°F. or until juice begins to bubble. Cool; cut into squares.

*Necessary to change temperature on LOW MIX.

Per Serving:			
Calories:	230	Fat:	13 g.
Protein:	3 g.	Cholesterol:	47 mg.
Carbohydrate:	26 g.	Sodium:	161 mg.

Coconut Oatmeal Pie ▶

 3 eggs, well beaten
 1 cup packed brown sugar
⅔ cup granulated sugar
⅔ cup quick-cooking oats
⅔ cup shredded coconut
½ cup milk
 2 tablespoons margarine or butter, melted
 1 teaspoon vanilla
½ cup broken pecans
 1 9-inch unbaked pie shell

Makes 8 servings

Preheat oven to 450°F. Combine all ingredients except pecans in large bowl. Add pecans; mix well. Pour into pie shell. Place pie on broiling trivet. Bake at 450°F. 8 minutes, then bake 15 minutes on *LOW MIX, 375°F. or until set.

*Necessary to change temperature on LOW MIX.

Per Serving:			
Calories:	504	Fat:	25 g.
Protein:	7 g.	Cholesterol:	104 mg.
Carbohydrate:	66 g.	Sodium:	215 mg.

Fudge Brownie Pie

 ¼ cup margarine or butter
 ¾ cup packed brown sugar
 1 tablespoon instant espresso coffee
 3 eggs
 1 bag (12 ounces) semisweet chocolate chips
 ¼ cup all-purpose flour
 1 cup chopped pecans
 1 9-inch unbaked pie shell
1½ teaspoons rum extract
 1 cup whipping cream, whipped stiffly
   Chocolate sprinkles

Makes 12 servings

Cream margarine and brown sugar until light and fluffy. Stir in espresso. Add eggs, one at a time, beating well after each.

Place chips in 4-cup measure or small bowl. Microwave at MEDIUM (50%) until melted, 1 to 2 minutes, sitrring 2 or 3 times. Stir chocolate, flour and pecans into butter, sugar, egg mixture. Pour into pie shell.

Bake 25 to 30 minutes on broiling trivet on LOW MIX. Cool. Fold rum extract into whipped cream. Spread on top of pie and decorate with sprinkles.

Per Serving:			
Calories:	480	Fat:	35 g.
Protein:	5 g.	Cholesterol:	96 mg.
Carbohydrate:	42 g.	Sodium:	168 mg.

◀ Nut Cake With Mocha Frosting

  8 eggs
1½ cups sugar
  2 cups hazelnuts or walnuts
 ¼ cup all-purpose flour
1½ tablespoons baking powder

Frosting:
  1 pint heavy cream
 ½ cup plus 2 tablespoons sugar
 ¼ cup plus 1 tablespoon
     chocolate-flavor
     drink mix
2½ teaspoons vanilla
  1 teaspoon instant coffee

Makes 10 servings

Grease and flour two 9-inch round cake pans; line with wax paper. Combine eggs and sugar in blender; blend until light and fluffy. Add nuts; blend until finely chopped. Add flour and baking powder; blend until just mixed. Pour into prepared pans. Bake 20 to 25 minutes on LOW MIX. If wooden pick inserted in center does not come out clean, let stand in oven a few minutes to complete cooking. Cool.

For frosting, combine remaining ingredients in medium bowl. Beat until stiff. Frost cake and chill. Cake must be refrigerated.

Per Serving:	
Calories:	561
Protein:	9 g.
Carbohydrate:	52 g.
Fat:	37 g.
Cholesterol:	285 mg.
Sodium:	216 mg.

Strawberry Puff Ring

½ cup water
2 tablespoons plus 1½ teaspoons margarine or butter
½ cup all-purpose flour
3 eggs
2 cups prepared vanilla pudding or 2 cups sweetened whipped cream
1 pint strawberries, rinsed, hulled and sliced
Powdered sugar

Makes 8 servings

Place water and margarine in medium bowl. Microwave at HIGH (100%) until boiling, about 2 minutes. Blend in flour until smooth. Microwave at HIGH (100%) 1 minute. Add eggs, 1 at a time, beating well after each. Preheat oven to 400°F. Drop dough by tablespoonfuls into 8 equal puffs touching each other in 8-inch circle onto greased round baking pan.

Bake 25 minutes at 400°F. Prick puff with sharp knife in several places to allow steam to escape. Let stand in oven 5 minutes; remove from oven to cool. Cut cooled puff ring in half. Spoon pudding into bottom half of ring; top with strawberries. Replace top half. Sprinkle with powdered sugar.

Per Serving:			
Calories:	186	Fat:	8 g.
Protein:	6 g.	Cholesterol:	111 mg.
Carbohydrate:	25 g.	Sodium:	152 mg.

Preserve Cake ▾

3 cups all-purpose flour
1 teaspoon baking soda
½ teaspoon ground allspice
½ teaspoon ground cinnamon
½ teaspoon ground nutmeg
2 cups sugar
¾ cup margarine or butter, softened
4 eggs
1 cup buttermilk
½ teaspoon vanilla
2 cups preserves (combine 2 or more flavors)
2 cups chopped pecans

Makes 12 servings

Mix flour, baking soda, allspice, cinnamon and nutmeg. Set aside. Beat sugar and margarine until light and fluffy. Add eggs, 1 at a time, beating well after each. Stir in flour mixture alternately with buttermilk, beating well after each addition until smooth. Mix vanilla, preserves and pecans together. Fold mixture into batter until thoroughly blended.

Pour into greased 10-inch tube pan. Bake 50 minutes on LOW MIX. If wooden pick inserted in center does not come out clean, let stand in oven a few minutes to complete cooking. Cool 10 minutes; remove from pan. Cool completely on wire rack.

Per Serving:			
Calories:	647	Fat:	27 g.
Protein:	8 g.	Cholesterol:	92 mg.
Carbohydrate:	97 g.	Sodium:	278 mg.

Sour Cream Pound Cake

4 cups all-purpose flour
2 teaspoons baking powder
1 teaspoon baking soda
½ teaspoon salt
2 cups sugar
1 cup margarine or butter, softened
4 eggs
1 teaspoon vanilla
2 cups dairy sour cream
½ cup sugar
¼ cup finely chopped walnuts
2 tablespoons ground cinnamon

Makes 12 servings

Mix flour, baking powder, baking soda and salt in medium bowl. Set aside. Beat 2 cups sugar and the margarine until light and fluffy. Add eggs, one at a time, beating well after each. Mix in vanilla. Stir in flour mixture alternately with sour cream, beating after each addition until smooth. Set aside.

Combine ½ cup sugar, the nuts and cinnamon. Pour half the batter into well-greased 10-inch tube pan; sprinkle with half of filling. Repeat with remaining batter and filling.

Bake 45 minutes on LOW MIX. If wooden pick inserted in center does not come out clean, let stand in oven a few minutes to complete cooking. Cool 10 minutes; remove from pan. Cool completely on wire rack.

Per Serving:			
Calories:	586	Fat:	28 g.
Protein:	8 g.	Cholesterol:	109 mg.
Carbohydrate:	77 g.	Sodium:	456 mg.

Classic Cranberry Tea Cake

¾ cup margarine or butter, softened
1½ cups sugar
3 eggs
2½ teaspoons almond extract
3 cups all-purpose flour
1½ teaspoons baking powder
1½ teaspoons baking soda
¾ teaspoon salt
1½ cups sour cream
¾ cup canned whole berry cranberry sauce

Makes 16 servings

Thoroughly grease and flour 12-cup fluted bundt cake pan. With an electric mixer, beat margarine. Gradually add sugar and beat until fluffy. Add eggs, one at a time, beating well after each addition. Add extract.

Sift dry ingredients together and add alternately with the sour cream. Fold in cranberries.

Pour into prepared pan and bake on broiling trivet on LOW MIX 35 to 45 minutes or until wooden pick inserted in center comes out clean. Allow to cool on counter 30 minutes. Turn out onto plate and allow to finish cooling before glazing.

Glaze:

¾ cup powdered sugar
½ teaspoon almond extract
2 teaspoons warm water
¼ cup toasted sliced almonds

Combine first 3 ingredients. Drizzle on cake and top with almonds.

Per Serving:			
Calories:	350	Fat:	16 g.
Protein:	5 g.	Cholesterol:	62 mg.
Carbohydrate:	48 g.	Sodium:	360 mg.

Biscuits ▲

5 cups all-purpose flour
3 tablespoons baking powder
3 tablespoons sugar
1 teaspoon salt
1 teaspoon baking soda
1 cup vegetable shortening
2 packages active dry yeast
2 to 4 tablespoons warm water
2 cups buttermilk

Makes 7 dozen biscuits

Combine dry ingredients. Cut in shortening until mixture resembles coarse crumbs. Dissolve yeast in warm water. Add dissolved yeast and buttermilk to dry ingredients; mix well. Roll out desired amount on lightly floured surface to a little over ¼ inch thick. Cut with floured 2-inch biscuit cutter.

Preheat oven to 400°F. Place biscuits on lightly greased baking pans. Let rise 10 minutes. Bake at 400°F. 10 to 12 minutes or until golden brown.

Note: Dough can be refrigerated 1 week in an air-tight plastic bag.

Per Serving:			
Calories:	54	Fat:	3 g.
Protein:	1 g.	Cholesterol:	—
Carbohydrate:	7 g.	Sodium:	78 mg.

Beer Muffins

4 cups buttermilk baking mix
1 can (12 ounces) beer
2 tablespoons sugar

Makes 1 dozen muffins

Preheat oven to 400°F. Combine all ingredients in large bowl. Spoon batter into two 6-cup greased medium muffin pans.

Bake 15 to 20 minutes at *LOW MIX 400°F. or until golden brown.

*Necessary to change temperature on LOW MIX.

Per Serving:			
Calories:	200	Fat:	6 g.
Protein:	3 g.	Cholesterol:	—
Carbohydrate:	30 g.	Sodium:	520 mg.

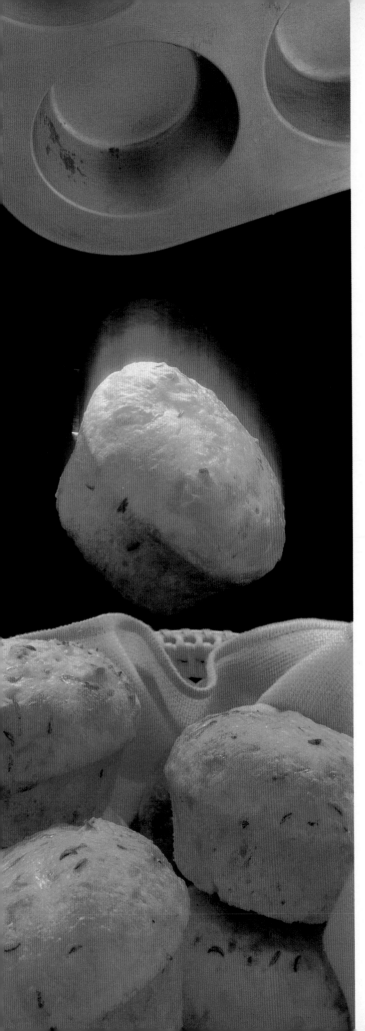

◀ Caraway Rolls

1 package active dry yeast
¼ cup warm water
1 cup cottage cheese
2 tablespoons sugar
1 tablespoon caraway seed
1 teaspoon salt
¼ teaspoon baking soda
1 egg, slightly beaten
2 cups all-purpose flour

Makes 1 dozen rolls

Dissolve yeast in warm water in large bowl. Microwave cottage cheese at HIGH (100%) until cheese is lukewarm, about 20 seconds; add to yeast mixture. Stir in sugar, caraway seed, salt, soda and egg. Slowly add flour, mixing until dough cleans bowl.

Cover with damp cloth. Place in oven. Let rise at 100°F. until double in bulk, 30 to 45 minutes. Stir down dough. Divide among two 6-cup greased medium muffin pans. Let rise at 100°F. until double in bulk, about 20 minutes.

Bake 15 minutes on LOW MIX or until tops spring back when touched lightly with finger.

Per Serving:			
Calories:	116	Fat:	2 g.
Protein:	5 g.	Cholesterol:	26 mg.
Carbohydrate:	19 g.	Sodium:	287 mg.

Zucchini Muffins

1½ cups all-purpose flour
½ cup sugar
1 teaspoon baking powder
½ teaspoon ground cinnamon
½ teaspoon salt
1 cup grated zucchini
½ cup chopped walnuts
½ cup raisins
1 egg
⅓ cup vegetable oil

Makes 1 dozen muffins

Combine dry ingredients in medium bowl. Mix in remaining ingredients until just moistened. Spoon batter into greased medium muffin pans.

Bake 20 to 24 minutes on *LOW MIX 400°F., or until tops spring back when touched lightly with finger.

*Necessary to change temperature on LOW MIX.

Per Serving:			
Calories:	204	Fat:	10 g.
Protein:	3 g.	Cholesterol:	23 mg.
Carbohydrate:	26 g.	Sodium:	125 mg.

Chocolate Chip Banana Crumb Loaf ▲

1 package (14 ounces) banana bread mix or
  banana muffin mix
¾ cup semisweet chocolate mini morsels
  Ingredients to complete mix

Crumb Topping:
½ cup chopped walnuts
½ cup all-purpose flour
2 tablespoons granulated sugar
2 tablespoons packed brown sugar
¼ cup margarine or butter

Makes 12 servings

Grease and flour 9 × 5-inch loaf pan. For easy removal of finished loaf, place a 2½ × 16-inch strip of wax paper lengthwise in pan with both ends extending above top of pan.

Combine mix and morsels. Prepare bread mix according to package directions or muffin mix according to loaf pan directions. Pour into prepared pan. Combine remaining dry ingredients in small bowl. Cut in margarine until mixture resembles coarse crumbs. Top batter with this mixture.

Bake 35 to 45 minutes on broiling trivet on LOW MIX. If wooden pick inserted in center does not come out clean, let stand in oven a few minutes to complete cooking. Cool 5 minutes; remove from pan by lifting both ends of wax paper. Cool completely on wire rack.

Per Serving:			
Calories:	338	Fat:	19 g.
Protein:	4 g.	Cholesterol:	46 mg.
Carbohydrate:	40 g.	Sodium:	245 mg.

Apricot Pecan Oat Bran Muffins

¾ cup whole wheat flour
1 cup oat bran
¼ cup wheat germ
2 teaspoons baking powder
½ cup orange juice
¼ cup packed brown sugar
1 cup dried apricots, chopped
1 teaspoon grated orange peel
2 tablespoons vegetable oil
½ cup buttermilk
2 eggs
⅓ cup chopped pecans

Makes 1 dozen muffins

Combine whole wheat flour, oat bran, wheat germ and baking powder; set aside.

Place orange juice in small bowl. Microwave at HIGH (100%) 1 minute. Add brown sugar, apricots and orange peel. Cool slightly.

Preheat oven to 400°F. Combine oil, buttermilk and eggs in large bowl. Add apricot, orange and flour mixture. Stir just to combine ingredients.

Spoon batter into two 6-cup greased muffin pans. Sprinkle with pecans.

Bake 15 to 20 minutes at 400°F. or until tops spring back when touched lightly with finger.

Per Serving:			
Calories:	158	Fat:	6 g.
Protein:	5 g.	Cholesterol:	46 mg.
Carbohydrate:	25 g.	Sodium:	76 mg.

No-Knead Cheddar Dill Bread

2½ to 3 cups all-purpose flour
1 tablespoon sugar
2 teaspoons dill weed
1 teaspoon dill seed
1 teaspoon salt
¼ teaspoon baking soda
1 package active dry yeast
1 cup small-curd cottage cheese
¼ cup water
1 tablespoon margarine or butter
1 egg
2 cups shredded sharp Cheddar cheese
1 egg, slightly beaten
   Poppy seed

Makes one 8-inch round loaf,
16 servings

Combine 1 cup of flour, sugar, dill weed, dill seed, salt, baking soda and dry yeast in large mixing bowl.

Combine cottage cheese, water and margarine in 2-cup glass measure. Microwave at HIGH (100%) 2 minutes. Add cottage cheese mixture, egg and Cheddar cheese to dry ingredients. Stir well. Add enough flour to make a stiff dough.

Soak a cloth with hot water, wring it out and place it over mixing bowl. Let dough rise in oven at *SLOW COOK 100°F. until double in size, about 1 hour.

Grease well an 8-inch round cake pan. Place in pan bottom a wax paper circle cut to fit. Place a strip of wax paper, 2½ × 25 inches, around pan edge. Grease both wax paper circle and strip. Stir dough down and put in prepared pan, patting the dough to smooth it. Let dough rise in 100°F. oven until double in size, 35 to 45 minutes.

Brush bread lightly with beaten egg and sprinkle top with poppy seed. Bake 25 to 35 minutes on broiling trivet on LOW MIX. Remove from pan. Cool on wire rack.

*Necessary to change temperature on SLOW COOK.

Per Serving:			
Calories:	168	Fat:	7 g.
Protein:	8 g.	Cholesterol:	51 mg.
Carbohydrate:	17 g.	Sodium:	319 mg.

Hearty Cheese Caraway Bread

6¾ cups all-purpose flour
3 tablespoons sugar
2½ teaspoons salt
¼ teaspoon baking soda
1 package rapid rise yeast
2 teaspoons caraway seed
1 cup milk
1 cup water
⅓ cup margarine or butter
1¾ cups grated sharp Cheddar cheese
¼ cup melted margarine or butter (for greasing)

Makes 2 loaves,
24 servings

Set aside 1 cup of flour. In large bowl, mix remaining flour, sugar, salt, baking soda, yeast and caraway seed. Heat milk, water and ⅓ cup of margarine until hot to touch, approximately 2½ to 3 minutes on MEDIUM (50%); stir into dry ingredients. Mix in only enough reserved flour to make soft dough. Turn out onto lightly floured surface; knead until smooth and elastic, about 8 to 10 minutes. Cover; let rise 10 minutes.

Divide dough in half; roll half into a 15 × 9-inch rectangle. Sprinkle ¾ cup of grated cheese evenly over dough. Roll tightly from short end to other. Pinch dough together at ends and along seam. Repeat with second half of dough.

Brush tops of loaves with melted margarine and sprinkle top with 2 tablespoons from the remaining cheese. Press gently on top of loaves. Place each loaf in a buttered 8½ × 4½ × 2-inch loaf pan. Let rise in oven on *SLOW COOK 100°F. 40 minutes.

Bake 25 to 30 minutes on LOW MIX until golden brown. Remove from pans and cool on wire racks.

*Necessary to change temperature on SLOW COOK.

Per Serving:			
Calories:	216	Fat:	8 g.
Protein:	6 g.	Cholesterol:	9 mg.
Carbohydrate:	30 g.	Sodium:	343 mg.

◄ Onion-Cheese Bread

½ cup chopped onion (about 1 medium)
1 tablespoon margarine or butter
1½ cups buttermilk baking mix
½ cup milk
1 egg, well beaten
½ cup shredded sharp Cheddar cheese
2 tablespoons snipped parsley or 1 tablespoon dried parsley flakes
2 tablespoons margarine or butter
½ cup shredded sharp Cheddar cheese

Makes 8 servings

Combine onion and 1 tablespoon margarine in small bowl. Microwave at HIGH (100%) until onion is tender, about 2 minutes. Set onion aside.

Preheat oven to 400°F. Mix baking mix, milk and egg until just moistened in medium bowl. Stir in onion, ½ cup cheese and the parsley. Spread in greased square baking pan, 8 × 8 inches. Dot with 2 tablespoons margarine; sprinkle with ½ cup cheese. Bake at 400°F. until wooden pick inserted in center comes out clean, about 20 minutes.

Per Serving:	
Calories:	210
Protein:	7 g.
Carbohydrate:	15 g.
Fat:	14 g.
Cholesterol:	50 mg.
Sodium:	422 mg.

SNACKS & APPETIZERS

Your microwave oven makes it quick and easy to turn out appetizers that set the mood for the meal ahead. These timesaving recipes adapt well to advance planning and preparing or spur-of-the-moment snacks.

Light and Easy Clam Dip & Liver Pâté, page 26

Light and Easy Clam Dip

4 ounces light cream cheese
1 can (6½ ounces) minced clams, drained
¼ cup plain low-fat yogurt
¼ cup chopped onion
1 teaspoon prepared horseradish
1 teaspoon Worcestershire sauce

Makes 10 servings

Place cheese in small baking dish. Microwave at MEDIUM (50%) 45 seconds to 1 minute 15 seconds, stirring after half the time. Stir in remaining ingredients. Microwave at MEDIUM (50%) until heated through, 3½ to 5½ minutes, stirring after half the cooking time. Serve hot or cold with assorted fresh vegetables.

Per Serving:			
Calories:	44	Fat:	3 g.
Protein:	3 g.	Cholesterol:	15 mg.
Carbohydrate:	1 g.	Sodium:	67 mg.

Liver Pâté

1 pound chicken livers, rinsed and drained
2 cloves garlic, minced
1 small onion, chopped
2 tablespoons white wine or water
½ teaspoon dried parsley flakes
½ teaspoon salt (optional)
½ teaspoon pepper
1 hard-cooked egg, chopped
1 tablespoon brandy

Makes 16 servings

Combine livers, garlic, onion, wine and seasonings in 2-quart casserole. Cover. Microwave at HIGH (100%) until meat is no longer pink, 5 to 8 minutes, stirring once. Drain well. Place cooked livers, egg and brandy in blender or food processor. Purée until smooth. Turn into serving dish and chill. Pipe or spoon pâté on melba toast, cherry tomatoes or celery sticks.

Per Serving:			
Calories:	46	Fat:	1 g.
Protein:	6 g.	Cholesterol:	142 mg.
Carbohydrate:	1 g.	Sodium:	27 mg.

Tangy Vegetable Dip

¼ cup finely chopped carrot
¼ cup finely chopped green pepper
2 tablespoons finely chopped onion
2 tablespoons water
1 cup low-fat cottage cheese
¼ cup plain low-fat yogurt
2 tablespoons fresh lemon juice
2 teaspoons dried dill weed
¼ teaspoon garlic powder
¼ teaspoon paprika
⅛ teaspoon cayenne pepper
1 large carrot, cut into 4 × ½-inch spears
1 medium cucumber, cut into 4 × ½-inch spears
1 medium jicama, cut into 4 × ½-inch spears or medium green pepper, cut into strips

Makes 12 servings

Combine carrot, green pepper, onion and water in 1-quart casserole. Cover. Microwave at HIGH (100%) until vegetables are tender-crisp, 2 to 3 minutes, stirring once. Drain. Set aside.

Place cottage cheese, yogurt and lemon juice in food processor or blender. Process until smooth. Place in small bowl. Add cooked vegetables and dill weed. Mix well. Cover with plastic wrap and chill.

Combine garlic powder, paprika and cayenne in small bowl. Arrange vegetables on serving platter. Sprinkle with spice mixture. Serve vegetables with dip.

Per Serving:			
Calories:	36	Fat:	1 g.
Protein:	3 g.	Cholesterol:	2 mg.
Carbohydrate:	5 g.	Sodium:	84 mg.

Miniature Pizzas

¼ cup prepared pizza sauce
2 English muffins, split and crisply toasted
¼ cup chopped pepperoni
½ cup shredded mozzarella cheese
(about 2 ounces)
4 teaspoons grated Parmesan cheese

Makes 16 servings

Spread one-fourth of sauce on each muffin half. Top each with one-fourth of the pepperoni. Place 2 tablespoons mozzarella on each muffin half; sprinkle with Parmesan. Place on single layer of paper towels on turntable or on double layer of paper towels on dinner plate.

Microwave at HIGH (100%) until cheese is melted and filling is heated through, 1½ to 2 minutes. Cut each muffin half into 4 wedges.

Per Serving:			
Calories:	37	Fat:	2 g.
Protein:	2 g.	Cholesterol:	4 mg.
Carbohydrate:	4 g.	Sodium:	97 mg.

◄ Buffalo Chicken Wings

12 chicken wings
1 tablespoon garlic powder
2 teaspoons onion powder
4 tablespoons oil
2 tablespoons catsup
1 tablespoon honey
4 teaspoons hot sauce
1 teaspoon liquid smoke
2 teaspoons chili powder

Makes 6 servings

Separate chicken wings at joints into 3 parts each, discarding tips. Arrange on double layer of paper towels around outer edge of turntable or on roasting rack. Mix remaining ingredients.

Baste with ¾ of sauce mixture. Cover with wax paper. Microwave at HIGH (100%) for 6 minutes. Rearrange pieces and baste with remaining sauce. Microwave at HIGH (100%) until juices run clear, 4 to 6 minutes.

Per Serving:			
Calories:	304	Fat:	22 g.
Protein:	19 g.	Cholesterol:	57 mg.
Carbohydrate:	6 g.	Sodium:	212 mg.

Cheese Toasties ▲

4 slices bacon
1 cup shredded Cheddar cheese (about 4 ounces)
1 tablespoon mayonnaise or salad dressing
1 tablespoon finely chopped onion
1 teaspoon milk
½ teaspoon Worcestershire sauce
¼ teaspoon dry mustard
Dash of paprika
Dash of garlic powder
2 English muffins, split and crisply toasted

Makes 8 servings

Place bacon on triple thickness of paper towels. Cover with paper towel. Microwave at HIGH (100%) until bacon is evenly browned, 3 to 4 minutes; set aside.

Mix cheese, mayonnaise, onion, milk, Worcestershire sauce, mustard, paprika and garlic powder. Spread 2 tablespoons on each muffin half. Crumble 1 piece of bacon on top of each.

Place muffins around outer edge of turntable, leaving center empty or on double thickness of paper towels on dinner plate. Microwave at MEDIUM-HIGH (70%) until cheese melts, 1 to 2 minutes. Cut each muffin half into 4 wedges.

Per Serving:			
Calories:	126	Fat:	8 g.
Protein:	6 g.	Cholesterol:	19 mg.
Carbohydrate:	8 g.	Sodium:	152 mg.

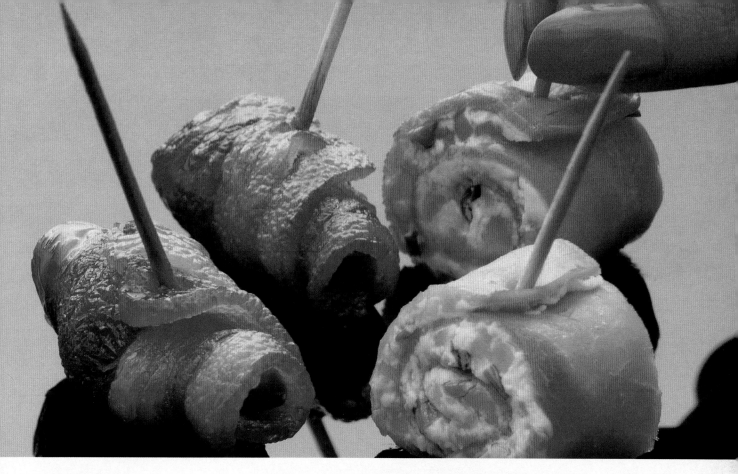

Rumaki ▲

3/4 cup soy sauce
1/4 cup dry sherry
1/2 cup packed brown sugar
1/8 teaspoon ground ginger
1/2 pound chicken livers, halved
12 to 13 slices bacon, halved
1 can (8 ounces) water chestnuts,
   drained and halved

Makes 8 servings

Mix soy sauce, sherry, brown sugar and ginger in 8 X 8-inch dish. Add chicken livers and marinate in refrigerator, covered, 2 hours; drain.

Place half of bacon on paper towels on paper plate. Cover with additional paper towel and microwave at HIGH (100%) until partially cooked, 2 to 3 minutes. Set aside. Repeat with remaining bacon.

Wrap a piece of chicken liver and a water chestnut slice in each bacon piece. Secure with wooden pick.

Place rumaki on double layer of paper towels around outer edge of turntable or 12-inch round glass dish. Cover with paper towel and microwave at HIGH (100%) until livers are cooked, 6 to 8 minutes, rearranging after half the time.

Per Serving:			
Calories:	127	Fat:	6 g.
Protein:	9 g.	Cholesterol:	133 mg.
Carbohydrate:	9 g.	Sodium:	575 mg.

Ham Roll-Ups ▲

1 package (3 ounces) cream cheese
1/2 cup shredded Cheddar cheese (about
   2 ounces)
1 tablespoon chopped green onion
1/2 teaspoon prepared mustard
4 slices fully cooked ham

Makes 8 servings

Microwave cream cheese in small bowl at HIGH (100%) until softened, 10 to 15 seconds. Stir in Cheddar cheese, green onion and mustard.

Spread cheese mixture on ham slices. Roll ham from narrow end. Cut each roll into 4 pieces; secure with wooden pick. Place on paper towels on turntable or large dinner plate. Microwave at HIGH (100%) 45 seconds to 2 minutes.

Per Serving:			
Calories:	76	Fat:	6 g.
Protein:	4 g.	Cholesterol:	23 mg.
Carbohydrate:	1 g.	Sodium:	166 mg.

29

◀ Stuffed Mushrooms

12 medium mushrooms
   (about 8 ounces)
 3 slices bacon, chopped
⅓ cup finely chopped
   green onions
¼ teaspoon salt
⅛ teaspoon pepper
 2 to 4 drops red pepper sauce
 1 tablespoon flour
¼ cup milk
 1 tablespoon shredded
   Cheddar cheese
 1 tablespoon shredded
   Monterey Jack cheese

Makes about 12 servings

Clean mushrooms. Remove stems and chop fine. Place mushroom caps on paper towels on turntable or dinner plate. Microwave at HIGH (100%) 45 seconds to 1 minute. Drain and set aside.

Place bacon in medium bowl. Microwave at HIGH (100%) until crisp, 2 to 3 minutes. Drain. Chop bacon, return to bowl and add chopped mushroom stems, onions, salt, pepper and red pepper sauce. Microwave at HIGH (100%) until mushrooms and onions are tender, 2 to 3 minutes.

Blend in flour, stir in milk until smooth. Microwave at HIGH (100%) until thickened and smooth, 30 seconds to 2 minutes, stirring once. Stir in cheeses.

Fill each mushroom cap with bacon mixture. Place around outer edge of turntable or 12-inch round glass plate lined with paper towels. Microwave at HIGH (100%) until cheese melts, 30 seconds to 1½ minutes.

Per Serving:
Calories:	32
Protein:	1 g.
Carbohydrate:	2 g.
Fat:	2 g.
Cholesterol:	4 mg.
Sodium:	86 mg.

Chicken Kabobs

1 pound boned chicken breasts,
    skinned and cut into
    1-inch cubes
¼ cup soy sauce
2 teaspoons sugar
¼ teaspoon salt
1 teaspoon garlic powder
¼ teaspoon ground ginger
    Dash of pepper
1 green pepper, cut into
    ½-inch cubes
15 medium mushrooms
    (about 4 ounces), halved
2 tablespoons honey

Makes 30 servings

Mix chicken pieces, soy sauce, sugar, salt, garlic powder, ginger and pepper. Let stand 10 to 20 minutes. Drain, reserving soy sauce mixture.

Alternate 1 green pepper cube, 1 chicken cube and 1 mushroom half on round wooden toothpicks. Place 15 kabobs on single layer of paper towels around outer edge of turntable or on roasting rack. Stir honey into reserved soy sauce mixture; brush each kabob generously.

Microwave, uncovered, at HIGH (100%) until chicken is tender and green peppers are tender-crisp, 2½ to 3½ minutes, brushing each kabob with soy sauce mixture after half the cooking time. Repeat with remaining kabobs.

Variation: Substitute 1 can (15 ounces) pineapple chunks (juice pack), drained, for mushrooms.

Per Serving:	
Calories:	26
Protein:	4 g.
Carbohydrate:	2 g.
Fat:	–
Cholesterol:	9 mg.
Sodium:	163 mg.

Party Mix ▲

½ cup margarine or butter
2 tablespoons Worcestershire
    sauce
3 to 5 drops red pepper sauce
2 cups bite-size shredded corn
    squares

2 cups bite-size shredded wheat
    squares
2 cups bite-size shredded rice
    squares
1 cup salted nuts
1 cup thin pretzel sticks

Makes 16 servings

Combine margarine, Worcestershire sauce and red pepper sauce in small bowl. Microwave at HIGH (100%) until margarine melts, 1 to 2 minutes. Stir to blend.

Combine remaining ingredients in 3-quart casserole. Add margarine mixture, tossing to blend. Microwave at HIGH (100%) until cereal is well coated and crisp, 5 to 6 minutes, stirring every minute. Spread evenly onto paper towel-lined tray or cookie sheet. Cool.

Per Serving:					
Calories:	180	Carbohydrate:	20 g.	Cholesterol:	—
Protein:	3 g.	Fat:	10 g.	Sodium:	348 mg.

◄ Mini Mexican Meatballs

- 1 pound ground beef
- 1 envelope (1¼ ounces) taco seasoning mix
- 1 egg
- 1 can (4 ounces) whole green chilies, chopped
- ½ cup chopped onion
- 1 tablespoon margarine or butter
- 1 tablespoon all-purpose flour
- ¾ cup milk
- 1 cup shredded Cheddar cheese (about 4 ounces)
- ½ cup shredded Monterey Jack cheese (about 2 ounces)
- 1 small coarsely chopped tomato Tortilla chips

Makes 8 servings

Mix ground beef, taco seasoning mix and egg. Shape into 1-inch balls; place in single layer in 10-inch pie plate. Microwave at HIGH (100%) until meatballs are firm and lose their pink color, 5½ to 6½ minutes, stirring once or twice during cooking. Drain, cover and set aside.

Combine green chilies, onion and margarine in 2-quart casserole. Microwave at HIGH (100%) until onions are tender, 1½ to 2½ minutes. Blend in flour; stir in milk until smooth. Microwave at HIGH (100%) until thickened, 2½ to 3½ minutes, stirring once or twice during cooking.

Stir in Cheddar cheese, Monterey Jack cheese and tomato. Microwave at MEDIUM-HIGH (70%) until cheese is melted and smooth, 1 to 2 minutes, stirring once or twice with a wire whisk. Add meatballs to cheese sauce. Serve with tortilla chips.

Per Serving:	
Calories:	262
Protein:	17 g.
Carbohydrate:	7 g.
Fat:	18 g.
Cholesterol:	85 mg.
Sodium:	546 mg.

Hot Cheese Dip ▲

1 package (8 ounces) process American cheese
  loaf, cubed
¼ cup finely chopped green pepper
¼ cup milk
2 drops red pepper sauce

Makes 12 servings

Mix all ingredients in 1-quart casserole. Microwave at
MEDIUM-HIGH (70%) until cheese melts, 5 to 6 minutes, stirring to blend well once or twice during cooking. Serve with corn chips or snack crackers, if desired.

Variation: Add 2 cans (6½ ounces each) minced clams,
drained, with other ingredients. Microwave as above.

Per Serving:			
Calories:	74	Fat:	6 g.
Protein:	4 g.	Cholesterol:	18 mg.
Carbohydrate:	1 g.	Sodium:	273 mg.

Nachos ▲

16 large tortilla chips
¾ cup shredded Monterey Jack cheese (about
  3 ounces)
¼ cup shredded Cheddar cheese (about 1 ounce)

Makes 16 appetizers

Spread tortilla chips on 10-inch wax paper-lined paper
plate. Sprinkle with cheeses. Microwave at MEDIUM
(50%) until melted, 1½ to 2½ minutes.

Per Serving:			
Calories:	40	Fat:	3 g.
Protein:	2 g.	Cholesterol:	6 mg.
Carbohydrate:	2 g.	Sodium:	62 mg.

Hot Crabmeat Dip

1 package (8 ounces) cream
  cheese
2 cans (6½ ounces each)
  crabmeat, rinsed, drained
  and cartilage removed
¼ cup mayonnaise or salad
  dressing
2 tablespoons lemon juice
1 tablespoon minced green
  onion
1 teaspoon Worcestershire
  sauce
⅛ teaspoon cayenne pepper

Makes 16 servings

Place cream cheese in medium bowl. Microwave at MEDIUM (50%) until
softened, 1 to 2 minutes, stirring once. Shred crabmeat; stir into cream cheese
with remaining ingredients.

Microwave at MEDIUM (50%) until dip is heated through, 4 to 7 minutes,
stirring once. Garnish with paprika and parsley sprig. Serve hot with fresh
vegetables or wheat crackers, if desired.

Per Serving:					
Calories:	91	Carbohydrate:	1 g.	Cholesterol:	32 mg.
Protein:	4 g.	Fat:	8 g.	Sodium:	117 mg.

Lasagna, page 45

MAIN DISHES

The question "what's for dinner?" is easily answered with the help of your Sharp Microwave Oven and these easy-to-prepare recipes. Microwaved meat, poultry and seafood dishes are tender, juicy and perfect for the after-school, after-work rush hour because they're simple and speedy to prepare.

Meat Roasting Chart

Cut	Cooking Preparation	Microwave Procedure	Internal Temp. at Removal	Internal Temp. after Standing
BEEF				
Rolled Rib Boneless (4-6 lbs.)	Meat roasting rack. Cover with plastic wrap. Turn over halfway through cooking time.	MED. (50%) Rare: 7-9 min. per lb. Med.: 9½-11 min. per lb. Well: 12-14 min. per lb.	120°F. 135°F. 150°F.	130°F. 145°F. 160°F.
Tenderloin (2-4 lbs.)	Meat roasting rack. Cover with plastic wrap. Turn over halfway through cooking time.	MED. (50%) Rare: 6-8 min. per lb. Med.: 8½-10 min. per lb. Well: 11-13 min. per lb.	120°F. 135°F. 150°F.	130°F. 145°F. 160°F.
Chuck or Pot Roast (cook in ½ cup liquid) (2-3 lbs.)	Large covered casserole. Turn over halfway through cooking time.	MED. (50%)	150°F.	160°F.
Without vegetables		21-24 min. per lb.		
With 3-4 cups cut-up vegetables		27-30 min. per lb.		
Eye of Round (2-3 lbs.)	Rack. Cover with plastic wrap. Turn over halfway through cooking time.	MED. (50%) Rare: 5-8 min. per lb. Med.: 7-10 min. per lb. Well: 9-11 min. per lb.	120°F. 135°F. 150°F.	130°F. 145°F. 160°F.
Ground Meat (to brown for casserole)	Casserole. Cover with plastic wrap. Stir halfway through cooking time.	HIGH (100%) 4-6 min. per lb.	155°F.	160°F.
Hamburgers (¼ lb. each) 2 patties 4 patties	Rack. Cover with wax paper. Turn over halfway through cooking time.	HIGH (100%) 3-4 min. 4-6 min.		

Cut	Cooking Preparation	Microwave Procedure	Internal Temp. at Removal	Internal Temp. after Standing
PORK				
Loin Roast	Meat roasting rack. Cover with plastic wrap. Turn over halfway through cooking time.	MED.-HIGH (70%) 7-11 min. per lb.	160°F.	170°F.
Boneless		MED. (50%) 12-14 min. per lb.	160°F.	170°F.
Tenderloin	Same procedure as above.	MED.-LOW (30%) 13-17 min. per lb.	160°F.	170°F.
Chops (1 inch thick) 2 chops	Preheated browning dish. Add margarine or butter for better browning. Turn over halfway through cooking time.	HIGH (100%) Med.: 3-4 min. Well: 4-5 min.	160°F. 170°F.	170°F. 180°F.
4 chops		Med.: 4-5 min. Well: 5-6 min.	160°F. 170°F.	170°F. 180°F.
Bacon 2 slices 4 slices 6 slices	Place bacon between paper towels on paper plate or on a rack.	HIGH (100%) 1½-2 min. 2½-3½ min. 3½-4½ min.		
Smoked Ham Canned Butt Shank	Casserole. Cover with plastic wrap. Turn over halfway through cooking time. Drain and shield if necessary.	MED. (50%) 5-8 min. per lb. 8-11 min. per lb.	130°F. 130°F.	135°F. 135°F.

Cut	Cooking Preparation	Microwave Procedure	Internal Temp. at Removal	Internal Temp. after Standing
LAMB				
Leg	Meat roasting rack. Cover with plastic wrap. Turn over halfway through cooking time.	MED. (50%) Rare: 5-8 min. per lb. Med.: 7-10 min. per lb. Well: 9-12 min. per lb.	120°F. 135°F. 150°F.	140°F. 150°F. 160°F.
Chops (1 inch thick) 2 chops 4 chops	Preheated browning dish. Add margarine or butter for better browning. Turn over halfway through cooking time.	HIGH (100%) Rare: 2-3 min. per lb. Med.: 3-4 min. per lb. Well: 4-5 min. per lb. Rare: 3-4 min. per lb. Med.: 4-5 min. per lb. Well: 5-6 min. per lb.	120°F. 135°F. 150°F. 120°F. 135°F. 150°F.	140°F. 150°F. 160°F. 140°F. 150°F. 160°F.

Poultry Roasting Chart

Cut	Cooking Preparation	Microwave Procedure	Internal Temp. at Removal	Internal Temp. after Standing
CHICKEN				
Whole	Breast side down on rack. Cover with plastic wrap. Turn over halfway through cooking time.	MED.-HIGH (70%) 5-8 min. per lb.	170°F.	180°F.
Pieces Bone-in Boneless	Rack. Cover with plastic wrap. Turn over halfway through cooking time.	HIGH (100%) 5-7½ min. per lb. 4-7 min. per lb.	170°F. 160°F.	180°F. 170°F.
TURKEY				
Whole (up to 10 lbs.)	Breast side down on rack. Cover with plastic wrap. Turn over halfway through cooking time.	MED. (50%) 10-14 min. per lb.	170°F.	180°F.
Breast Bone-in Boneless	Rack. Cover with plastic wrap. Turn over halfway through cooking time.	MED. (50%) 11-15 min. per lb. 14-18 min. per lb.	160°F. 160°F.	170°F. 170°F.
CORNISH HENS	Breast side down on rack. Cover with plastic wrap. Turn over halfway through cooking time.	MED.-HIGH (70%) 4-7 min. per lb.	170°F.	180°F.

Fish and Seafood Cooking Chart

Cut	Cooking Preparation	Microwave Procedure	Standing Time
FILLETS	Pie plate or casserole. Cover with plastic wrap.	MED.-HIGH (70%) 4-6 min. per lb.	3 min.
STEAKS	Pie plate or casserole. Cover with plastic wrap. Turn over halfway through cooking time.	MED.-HIGH (70%) 5-7 min. per lb.	3 min.
SHRIMP & SCALLOPS	Pie plate or casserole. Cover with plastic wrap. Turn over halfway through cooking time.	MED.-HIGH (70%) 4-6 min. per lb.	1-2 min.

MEATS

◄ Peppered Rib Roast

2 teaspoons coarsely ground pepper
¾ teaspoon garlic powder
½ teaspoon salt (optional)
4 to 6-lb. boneless beef rolled rib roast

Makes 12 servings

Combine all ingredients except roast in small bowl. Rub mixture on all sides of roast. Place roast fattiest side down on roasting rack. Estimate total cooking time; divide in half. (See chart page 36.)

Cover with vented plastic wrap. Microwave at MEDIUM (50%) first half of total cooking time. Turn roast fattiest side up. Re-cover.

Microwave at MEDIUM (50%) second half of cooking time or until internal temperature registers desired doneness. Let stand tented with foil 10 minutes before carving. (Internal temperature will rise 10 to 20°F. during standing time.)

Per Serving:			
Calories:	205	Fat:	13 g.
Protein:	21 g.	Cholesterol:	70 mg.
Carbohydrate:	–	Sodium:	60 mg.

Brown Gravy ◄

2 tablespoons fat
1 cup cooking liquid or beef broth
1 tablespoon all-purpose flour
  Salt and pepper

Makes 16 servings

After roasting meat, remove from baking dish; cover to keep warm and set aside. Pour cooking liquid from meat into bowl, leaving particles in baking dish. Allow fat to rise to the top. Return 2 tablespoons fat to the baking dish. Skim off any remaining fat and discard. Pour cooking liquid into 1-cup measure. If necessary, add beef broth to measure 1 cup. Set aside.

Blend flour into fat in baking dish. Microwave at HIGH (100%) until lightly browned, 3 to 7 minutes. Gradually stir in reserved cooking liquid. Microwave at HIGH (100%) until slightly thickened and smooth, 3 to 6 minutes, stirring several times during cooking. Sprinkle with salt and pepper to taste. Stir in a few drops brown bouquet sauce, if desired.

Per Serving:			
Calories:	18	Fat:	2 g.
Protein:	–	Cholesterol:	2 mg.
Carbohydrate:	–	Sodium:	49 mg.

Homestyle Chili

1½ pounds ground beef
1 large onion, chopped
3 cloves garlic, minced
2 stalks celery, chopped
1 large green pepper, chopped
1 can (6 ounces) tomato paste
1 can (14 ounces) tomato puree
½ cup water
2 cans (16 ounces each) red kidney beans, drained
1 tablespoon chili powder
1 teaspoon cumin
1 teaspoon oregano
1 teaspoon salt
½ teaspoon cayenne pepper

Makes 6 servings

Cook ground beef in 4-quart casserole at HIGH (100%) until beef loses pink color, 6 to 9 minutes. Drain. Add remaining ingredients. Cover.

Microwave at HIGH (100%) until boiling, 8 to 10 minutes. Stir very well. Microwave at MEDIUM (50%) 45 to 55 minutes, until slightly thickened and tender, stirring several times during cooking.

Variation: Substitute 1½ pounds uncooked ground or chopped turkey for ground beef. This makes a lighter chili.

Per Serving:			
Calories:	415	Fat:	18 g.
Protein:	29 g.	Cholesterol:	69 mg.
Carbohydrate:	35 g.	Sodium:	1117 mg.

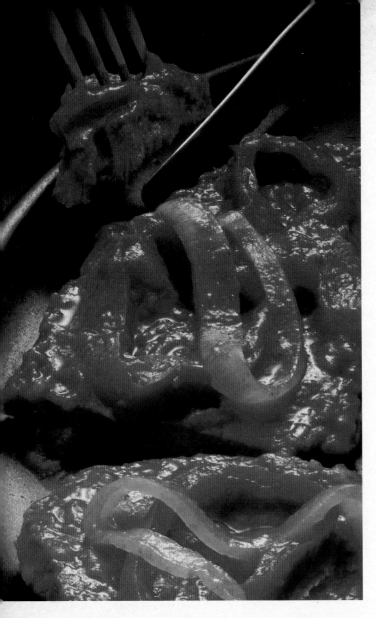

◀ Swiss Steak

2 pounds boneless beef round steak
¼ cup all-purpose flour
½ teaspoon salt
¼ teaspoon pepper
1 cup thinly sliced celery
1 medium onion, thinly sliced and separated into rings
1 medium green pepper, thinly sliced
1 can (10¾ ounces) condensed tomato soup
⅔ cup water
1 tablespoon Worcestershire sauce

Makes 8 servings

Trim round steak; pound well. Cut into 6 to 8 pieces. Mix flour, salt and pepper. Coat beef with flour mixture. Place meat and any remaining flour mixture in rectangular baking dish, 12 X 8 inches, or 10-inch square casserole.

Combine celery, onion and green pepper in medium bowl. Microwave at HIGH (100%) until vegetables are tender, 2 to 4 minutes. Mix with remaining ingredients. Pour over beef.

Microwave, covered, at HIGH (100%) 5 minutes. Reduce power to MEDIUM (50%). Microwave until beef is tender, 35 to 45 minutes, rearranging pieces after half the cooking time.

Per Serving:			
Calories:	243	Fat:	9 g.
Protein:	28 g.	Cholesterol:	82 mg.
Carbohydrate:	10 g.	Sodium:	476 mg.

Pot Roast

2 to 3-pound beef chuck roast, boneless
1 envelope (1.5 ounces) spaghetti sauce mix
¼ cup water
3 medium carrots, cut into 1-inch chunks
1 medium onion, cut into eighths
1 large potato, peeled and cut into eighths
1 package (10 ounces) frozen green peas, defrosted and drained

Makes 8 servings

Per Serving:			
Calories:	215	Fat:	5 g.
Protein:	26 g.	Cholesterol:	65 mg.
Carbohydrate:	16 g.	Sodium:	607 mg.

Pierce meat deeply and thoroughly on all sides with a fork. Place meat, sauce mix and water in a large oven cooking bag. Place in casserole. Secure bag with nylon tie. Make six ½-inch slits in neck of bag below tie.

Microwave at MEDIUM (50%) 30 minutes. Turn roast over; add vegetables except peas. Microwave 25 minutes to 1 hour or until meat and vegetables are fork-tender. Add peas the last 5 minutes of cooking time. Let stand, covered, 15 minutes, to tenderize further and develop flavor.

Beef with Peppers and Tomatoes ▲

¼ cup soy sauce
¼ cup water
2 tablespoons sherry
½ teaspoon garlic powder
2 pounds beef flank steak, cut across grain into thin strips
2 medium green peppers, thinly sliced
2 tablespoons cornstarch
½ cup cold water
1 tomato, cut into 16 wedges

Mix soy sauce, water, sherry, garlic powder and beef strips in plastic bag or medium bowl; close tightly or cover. Refrigerate 8 hours or overnight.

Combine green peppers, beef and marinade in 2-quart casserole; cover. Microwave at MEDIUM (50%) until beef is tender, 20 to 25 minutes, stirring after half the cooking time. Drain, reserving meat juices. Set beef mixture aside, covered.

Mix cornstarch and cold water in 2-cup measure or small bowl. Stir in reserved meat juices. Microwave at HIGH (100%) until sauce thickens, 2 to 3 minutes, stirring after half the cooking time. Stir sauce and tomatoes into beef and green pepper mixture; cover. Microwave at HIGH (100%) until tomatoes are heated through, 1 to 3 minutes.

Per Serving:			
Calories:	235	Fat:	13 g.
Protein:	23 g.	Cholesterol:	60 mg.
Carbohydrate:	5 g.	Sodium:	591 mg.

Savory Beef Burgundy

1 can (10¾ ounces) cream of mushroom soup
1 envelope (1 ounce) dried onion soup mix
1½ cups burgundy wine
1½ pounds sirloin steak, boneless, 1-inch cubes
10 ounces mushrooms, sliced
1 large onion, chopped

Makes 6 servings

Combine mushroom soup, dried soup mix and wine in a 3-quart casserole. Add beef, mushrooms and onion; mix well. Cover. Microwave at HIGH (100%) until boiling, 10 to 12 minutes. Stir well and re-cover. Microwave at MEDIUM (50%) until tender, 45 to 55 minutes, stirring several times during cooking. Serve over rice or noodles, if desired.

Variation: For Savory Beef Burgundy Stroganoff, stir 1 cup dairy sour cream into cooked mixture until well blended. Serve.

Per Serving:			
Calories:	342	Fat:	21 g.
Protein:	24 g.	Cholesterol:	77 mg.
Carbohydrate:	13 g.	Sodium:	880 mg.

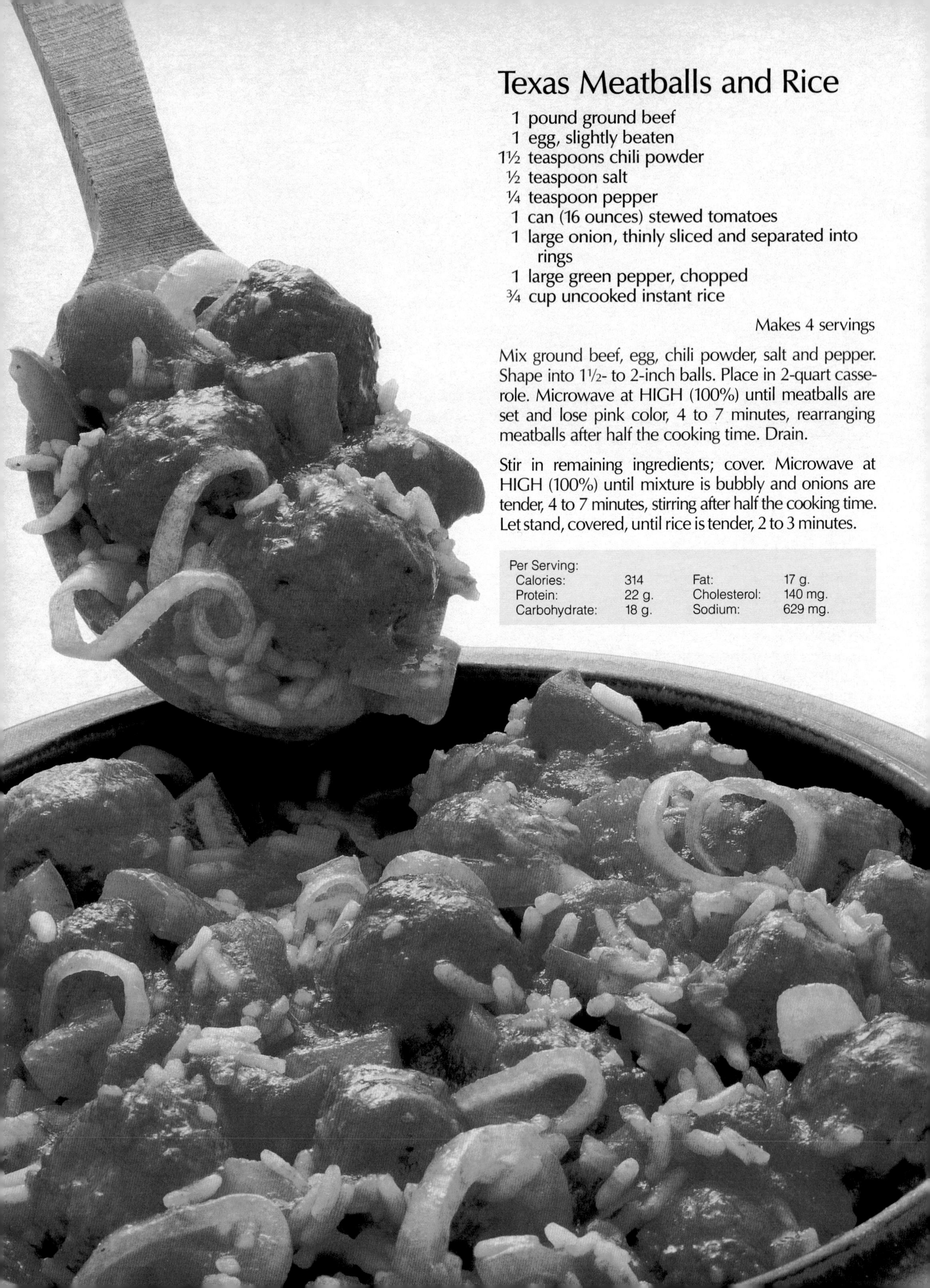

Texas Meatballs and Rice

- 1 pound ground beef
- 1 egg, slightly beaten
- 1½ teaspoons chili powder
- ½ teaspoon salt
- ¼ teaspoon pepper
- 1 can (16 ounces) stewed tomatoes
- 1 large onion, thinly sliced and separated into rings
- 1 large green pepper, chopped
- ¾ cup uncooked instant rice

Makes 4 servings

Mix ground beef, egg, chili powder, salt and pepper. Shape into 1½- to 2-inch balls. Place in 2-quart casserole. Microwave at HIGH (100%) until meatballs are set and lose pink color, 4 to 7 minutes, rearranging meatballs after half the cooking time. Drain.

Stir in remaining ingredients; cover. Microwave at HIGH (100%) until mixture is bubbly and onions are tender, 4 to 7 minutes, stirring after half the cooking time. Let stand, covered, until rice is tender, 2 to 3 minutes.

Per Serving:

Calories:	314	Fat:	17 g.
Protein:	22 g.	Cholesterol:	140 mg.
Carbohydrate:	18 g.	Sodium:	629 mg.

Dressed-Up Meat Loaf ▶

1½ pounds lean ground beef
½ cup soft bread crumbs
½ cup red wine
1 egg, beaten
2 tablespoons chopped onion
2 tablespoons chopped green pepper
1 teaspoon instant beef bouillon
½ teaspoon salt
½ teaspoon dry mustard
¼ teaspoon pepper

Makes 8 servings

Thoroughly blend all ingredients. Press into loaf dish, 9 × 5 inches. Microwave at HIGH (100%) until internal temperature reaches 155°F., 11 to 15 minutes. Let stand 3 to 5 minutes covered with aluminum foil. If desired, spread top of meat loaf with ¼ cup catsup during last 2 minutes of cooking time.

Per Serving:			
Calories:	174	Fat:	8 g.
Protein:	19 g.	Cholesterol:	94 mg.
Carbohydrate:	4 g.	Sodium:	245 mg.

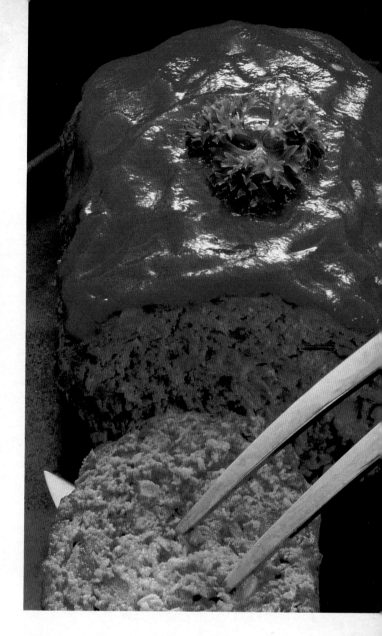

Spicy Couscous Pockets

1 can (16 ounces) whole tomatoes, drained
   (reserve juice)
½ cup couscous
1½ tablespoons chili powder
1 teaspoon ground cumin
1 teaspoon dried oregano leaves
1 pound lean ground beef
1 large onion, chopped
¼ cup chopped green pepper
1 clove garlic, minced
1 cup raisins
¾ teaspoon salt
¼ teaspoon pepper
12 mini whole wheat pita pockets
¼ cup snipped fresh parsley
1 pint plain yogurt

Makes 12 servings

Place reserved tomato juice in 4-cup measure. Add enough water to measure ⅔ cup. Microwave on HIGH (100%) until boiling, 1½ to 2 minutes. Add couscous, chili powder, cumin and oregano. Mix well. Cover and set aside.

Combine beef, onion, green pepper and garlic in 3-quart casserole. Microwave on HIGH (100%) until beef is no longer pink, 5 to 7 minutes, stirring once. Drain.

Add couscous mixture, tomatoes, raisins, salt and pepper. Mix well. Microwave on HIGH (100%) until hot, 7 to 9 minutes. Let stand 10 minutes.

Spoon beef mixture into warmed pita pockets. Stir parsley into yogurt. Top each pita with yogurt mixture.

Per Serving:			
Calories:	242	Fat:	5 g.
Protein:	14 g.	Cholesterol:	28 mg.
Carbohydrate:	36 g.	Sodium:	254 mg.

43

Swedish Meatballs ▲

1 pound ground beef
½ pound lean ground pork
½ cup dry bread crumbs
1 medium onion, chopped
⅓ cup milk
1 egg, beaten
½ teaspoon salt
¾ teaspoon ground allspice
¼ teaspoon ground nutmeg
¼ teaspoon pepper
2 tablespoons all-purpose flour
½ cup water
1 teaspoon instant beef bouillon
1 cup half-and-half or milk

Makes 6 servings

Per Serving:			
Calories:	317	Fat:	18 g.
Protein:	25 g.	Cholesterol:	138 mg.
Carbohydrate:	12 g.	Sodium:	383 mg.

Mix ground beef, ground pork, bread crumbs, onion, milk, egg, salt, allspice, nutmeg and pepper. Shape into 1- to 1½-inch balls. Place in single layer in rectangular baking dish, 12 × 8 inches, or 10-inch square casserole. Microwave at HIGH (100%) until meatballs are set and lose pink color, 8 to 10 minutes, rearranging after half the time.

Remove meatballs, reserving meat juices. Stir flour into meat juices. Stir in water and instant bouillon. Microwave at HIGH (100%) until slightly thickened, 3 to 4 minutes, stirring once or twice during cooking. Gradually blend in half-and-half. Reduce power to MEDIUM-HIGH (70%). Microwave until thickened and smooth, 3 to 5 minutes, stirring once or twice during cooking.

Stir meatballs into sauce until coated. Microwave at MEDIUM-HIGH (70%) until heated through, 1½ to 2 minutes.

Lasagna

1 pound ground beef
½ pound bulk hot or regular pork sausage
1 can (16 ounces) whole tomatoes
1 can (6 ounces) tomato paste
½ teaspoon salt
¼ teaspoon pepper
1 clove garlic, minced
1 carton (8 ounces) ricotta or creamed cottage cheese (about 1 cup)
1 egg, beaten
¼ cup grated Parmesan cheese
1 tablespoon dried parsley flakes
½ teaspoon dried oregano leaves
¼ teaspoon dried basil leaves
7 to 9 cooked lasagna noodles
1 cup shredded mozzarella cheese (about 4 ounces)

Makes 6 servings

Mix ground beef and sausage in 2-quart casserole. Microwave at HIGH (100%) until meat loses pink color, 5 to 9 minutes, stirring once to break up meat during cooking. Drain. Stir in tomatoes, tomato paste, salt, pepper and garlic. Microwave at HIGH (100%) until sauce thickens, 7 to 11 minutes, stirring occasionally.

While sauce is cooking, mix ricotta cheese, egg, Parmesan cheese, parsley, oregano and basil.

Layer one-third each of the noodles, meat sauce, ricotta cheese mixture and mozzarella in 12-inch square or round baking dish. Repeat twice, ending with mozzarella. Microwave at MEDIUM-HIGH (70%) until sauce bubbles, 10 to 16 minutes.

Per Serving:			
Calories:	478	Fat:	25 g.
Protein:	33 g.	Cholesterol:	133 mg.
Carbohydrate:	30 g.	Sodium:	1022 mg.

Sicilian Supper ▲

1 pound ground beef
½ cup chopped onion
½ cup chopped green pepper
1 package (8 ounces) cream cheese, cubed and softened
1 cup cooked egg noodles
1 can (6 ounces) tomato paste
½ cup water
½ cup milk
¼ teaspoon garlic salt
¼ teaspoon pepper
¼ cup grated Parmesan cheese

Makes 4 servings

Mix ground beef, onion and green pepper in 2-quart casserole. Microwave at HIGH (100%) until beef loses pink color, 5 to 9 minutes, stirring once to break up beef. Drain.

Stir in remaining ingredients except Parmesan. Microwave at HIGH (100%) 2 minutes. Reduce power to MEDIUM-HIGH (70%). Sprinkle with Parmesan. Microwave until heated through, 5 to 7 minutes.

Per Serving:			
Calories:	557	Fat:	39 g.
Protein:	30 g.	Cholesterol:	153 mg.
Carbohydrate:	23 g.	Sodium:	798 mg.

◄ South of the Border Eggplant

1 pound ground beef
4 slices bacon, cut into ½-inch pieces
½ cup chopped onion
½ cup chopped green pepper
1 clove garlic, minced
1 medium eggplant, cut into ½-inch cubes
(6 to 8 cups)
1 can (16 ounces) tomato sauce
¼ teaspoon pepper
1 cup shredded mozzarella cheese
(about 4 ounces)

Makes 6 servings

Place ground beef in medium bowl. Microwave at HIGH (100%) until beef loses pink color, 3 to 5 minutes, stirring to break up beef after half the cooking time. Drain and set aside.

Mix bacon, onion, green pepper and garlic in 10-inch square or round casserole. Microwave at HIGH (100%) until green pepper is tender and bacon is crisp, 4 to 6 minutes.

Stir in ground beef, eggplant, tomato sauce and pepper. Cover with plastic wrap. Microwave at HIGH (100%) until eggplant is tender, 11 to 15 minutes, stirring once or twice during cooking. Sprinkle with cheese. Microwave at HIGH (100%) until cheese melts, 45 seconds to 2 minutes.

Per Serving:			
Calories:	269	Fat:	16 g.
Protein:	21 g.	Cholesterol:	61 mg.
Carbohydrate:	12 g.	Sodium:	657 mg.

Stuffed Green Peppers

3 medium green peppers
1 pound lean ground beef
1 can (8 ounces) tomato sauce
½ cup uncooked instant rice
1 egg, slightly beaten
½ teaspoon dried oregano leaves
½ teaspoon salt
¼ teaspoon pepper
⅛ teaspoon garlic powder
¼ cup catsup or tomato sauce

Makes 6 servings

Cut green peppers in half lengthwise. Remove seeds and membranes. Set aside.

Mix ground beef, tomato sauce, rice, egg, oregano, salt, pepper and garlic powder. Spoon into pepper halves. Place on roasting rack. Cover loosely with wax paper.

Microwave at HIGH (100%) until green peppers are tender, 11 to 14 minutes. Rearrange peppers after half the cooking time. Top each green pepper half evenly with catsup during last 2 minutes of cooking.

Per Serving:					
Calories:	178	Carbohydrate:	11 g.	Cholesterol:	96 mg.
Protein:	17 g.	Fat:	7 g.	Sodium:	574 mg.

Fiesta Tamale Pie

- 1 pound ground beef
- ¼ pound bulk pork sausage
- ¼ cup chopped onion
- 1 clove garlic, minced
- 1 can (16 ounces) stewed tomatoes, drained
- 1 can (12 ounces) whole kernel corn, drained
- 1 can (6 ounces) tomato paste
- 1½ teaspoons chili powder
- ½ teaspoon salt
- ¼ cup sliced pitted ripe olives
- 1 package (8½ ounces) corn muffin mix
- 1 egg
- ⅓ cup milk
- ½ cup shredded Cheddar cheese (about 2 ounces)
- Dash of paprika

Makes 6 servings

Mix ground beef, sausage, onion and garlic in rectangular 12 X 8-inch baking dish or 10-inch square dish. Cover with wax paper and microwave at HIGH (100%) until meat loses pink color, 5 to 9 minutes, stirring once to break up meat. Drain. Stir in tomatoes, corn, tomato paste, chili powder and salt. Microwave at HIGH (100%) until mixture thickens, 4 to 6 minutes. Stir in olives.

Mix corn muffin mix, egg and milk until just moistened. Spread over meat mixture. Microwave at MEDIUM-HIGH (70%) 5 minutes. Increase power to HIGH (100%). Microwave until center is set, 5 to 8 minutes, sprinkling with cheese and paprika during last 2 minutes of cooking.

Per Serving:			
Calories:	505	Fat:	24 g.
Protein:	24 g.	Cholesterol:	139 mg.
Carbohydrate:	50 g.	Sodium:	1492 mg.

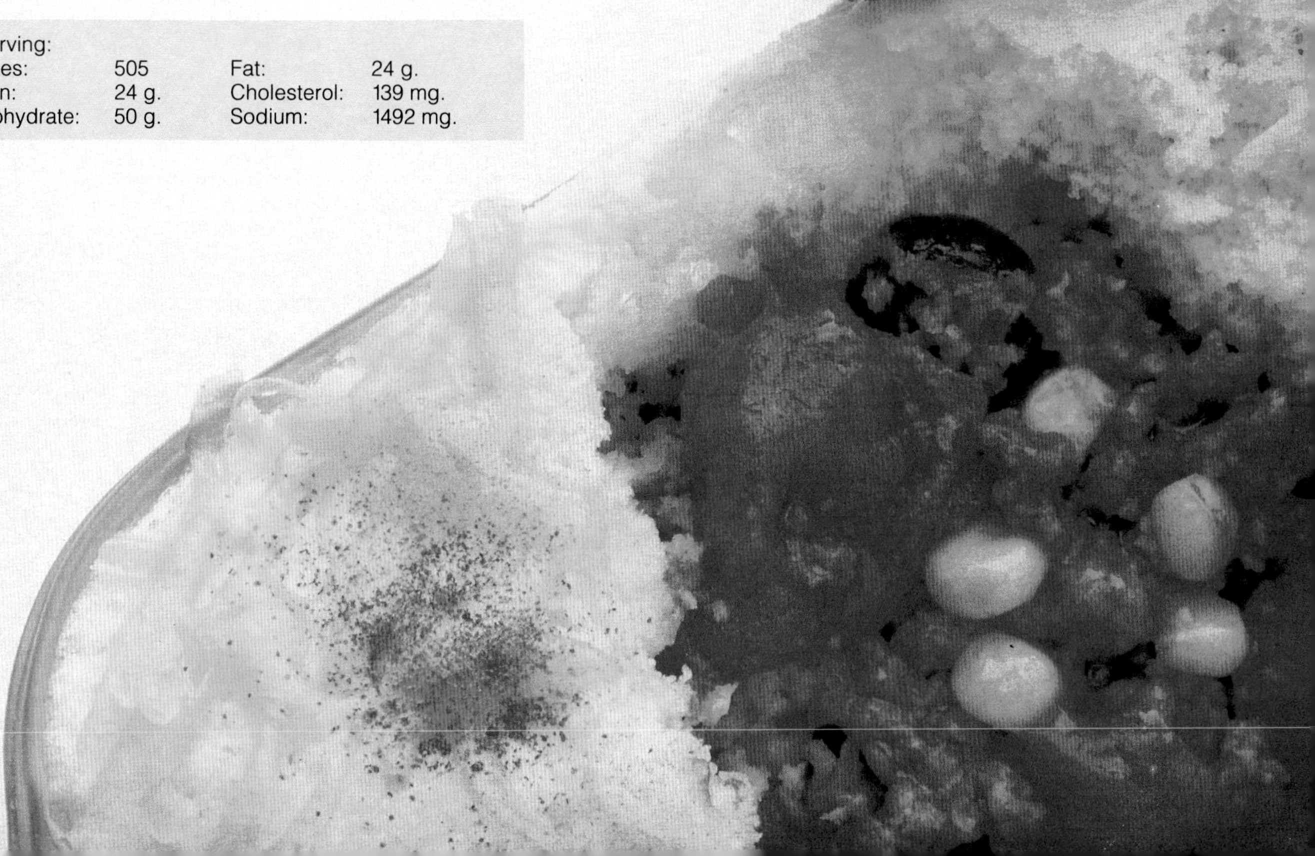

◄ Roast Loin of Pork with Apricot Glaze

1 cup coarsely chopped dried apricots
¾ cup orange juice
½ cup apricot nectar
    Juice and peel of ½ medium lemon, seeds removed
1 tablespoon honey
¼ teaspoon ground cinnamon
3½ pound boneless pork loin roast

Makes 8 to 10 servings

Mix all ingredients except pork roast in medium bowl or 4-cup measure. Microwave at HIGH (100%) until apricots are tender, 7 to 9 minutes, stirring 2 or 3 times during cooking. Remove lemon peel. Set glaze aside.

Place pork roast on roasting rack. Brush with half of the glaze. Place thin strips of aluminum foil over top of each end of roast. Microwave at MEDIUM (50%) until internal temperature reaches 160°F., 40 to 50 minutes, removing foil strips after first 15 minutes and basting 2 or 3 times with glaze during cooking.

Let stand loosely wrapped in aluminum foil until internal temperature reaches 170°F., 10 minutes. Spoon any remaining glaze over roast.

Per Serving:	
Calories:	340
Protein:	35 g.
Carbohydrate:	14 g.
Fat:	16 g.
Cholesterol:	108 mg.
Sodium:	84 mg.

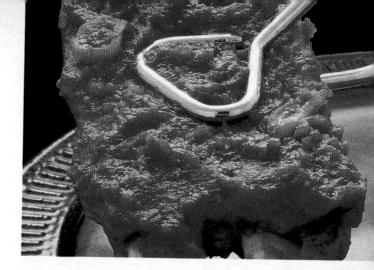

Applesauce-Barbecued Spareribs ▶

1 medium onion, thinly sliced and separated into rings
1 tablespoon margarine or butter
1 cup applesauce
½ cup catsup
2 tablespoons lemon juice
1 tablespoon Worcestershire sauce
½ teaspoon salt
⅛ teaspoon pepper
2½ pounds fresh pork spareribs, cut into 2- or 3-rib pieces

Makes 4 servings

Mix onion and margarine in a medium bowl. Microwave at HIGH (100%) until tender, 3 to 5 minutes. Stir in remaining ingredients except spareribs. Microwave at HIGH (100%) until hot and bubbly, 4 to 6 minutes, stirring 2 or 3 times during cooking. Set barbecue sauce aside.

Arrange spareribs in rectangular baking dish, 12 × 8 inches, or 10-inch square casserole. Spread with ¾ cup of the barbecue sauce. Cover with plastic wrap. Microwave at HIGH (100%) 5 minutes. Reduce power to MEDIUM (50%). Microwave 20 minutes. Rearrange and turn spareribs over. Re-cover.

Microwave at MEDIUM (50%) until fork-tender, 20 to 25 minutes. Drain. Spread remaining barbecue sauce over spareribs. Microwave, uncovered, at MEDIUM (50%) until barbecue sauce is hot and spareribs are glazed, 4 to 6 minutes.

Per Serving:			
Calories:	539	Fat:	37 g.
Protein:	33 g.	Cholesterol:	134 mg.
Carbohydrate:	18 g.	Sodium:	801 mg.

Pork Chops in Mustard Sauce

2 tablespoons margarine or butter
1 clove garlic, minced
1 medium onion, chopped
2 tablespoons flour
1 teaspoon or envelope instant chicken broth
½ cup water
¼ cup white wine
2 tablespoons prepared mustard
1 teaspoon Worcestershire sauce
¼ teaspoon salt
⅛ teaspoon pepper
4 ¾-inch thick pork chops (1½ pounds)
¼ cup heavy cream

Makes 4 servings

Pork Chops and Sauerkraut

1 can (16 ounces) sauerkraut, undrained
1 small onion, thinly sliced and separated into rings
4 pork chops, about ½ inch thick
½ teaspoon caraway seed
1 medium tart apple, cored and cut into thin rings

Makes 4 servings

Layer sauerkraut and onion in square baking dish, 8 × 8 inches. Top with pork chops. Sprinkle with caraway seed. Cover with wax paper.

Microwave at MEDIUM (50%) 10 minutes. Rearrange pork chops; top with apple. Cover. Microwave at MEDIUM (50%) until meat next to bone is no longer pink and apple rings are tender, 5 to 7 minutes.

Per Serving:			
Calories:	255	Fat:	12 g.
Protein:	25 g.	Cholesterol:	67 mg.
Carbohydrate:	11 g.	Sodium:	791 mg.

Combine margarine, garlic and onion in 3-quart casserole. Cover. Microwave at HIGH (100%) until tender, 3 to 5 minutes.

Add remaining ingredients, except for cream. Cover. Microwave at HIGH (100%) 5 minutes. Turn chops over and microwave at MEDIUM (50%) until meat is no longer pink, 8 to 10 minutes, turning over once. Place chops on serving platter and cover.

Add cream to sauce. Microwave at HIGH (100%) until heated through, 1 to 2 minutes. Pour over chops and serve immediately.

Per Serving:			
Calories:	538	Fat:	42 g.
Protein:	28 g.	Cholesterol:	118 mg.
Carbohydrate:	8 g.	Sodium:	880 mg.

Peppered Pork and Vegetables with Soft Noodles ▾

8 ounces medium egg noodles, cooked
1 tablespoon vegetable oil
1 cup diagonally sliced celery, ¼-inch slices
½ cup red or green pepper chunks, ¾-inch chunks
⅓ cup coarsely chopped onion
1 jar (7 ounces) sliced shiitake mushrooms, drained
1 jar (7 ounces) whole baby corn, drained
⅛ teaspoon sesame oil
1 pound boneless pork, trimmed and cut into thin strips

Sauce:
½ cup ready-to-serve chicken broth
¼ cup teriyaki sauce
1 tablespoon plus 1½ teaspoons cornstarch
¼ teaspoon pepper
¼ teaspoon sesame oil
⅛ teaspoon instant minced garlic

Makes 6 servings

Toss cooked egg noodles with 1 tablespoon vegetable oil. Cover to keep warm. Set aside. Combine celery, red pepper, onion and 1 tablespoon vegetable oil in 3-quart casserole. Cover. Microwave at HIGH (100%) until vegetables are tender-crisp, 3 to 4 minutes, stirring once.

Stir in mushrooms and corn. Set aside. Combine sesame oil and pork strips in 1-quart casserole. Microwave at HIGH (100%) until meat is no longer pink, about 3 to 5 minutes. Add pork strips to vegetable mixture. Set aside.

Combine all sauce ingredients in 2-cup measure. Mix well. Microwave at HIGH (100%) until sauce is thickened and translucent, 2 to 3½ minutes, stirring twice. Stir sauce into pork and vegetables. Add cooked egg noodles. Toss to combine. Cover. Microwave at HIGH (100%) until hot, 1 to 2 minutes.

Per Serving:			
Calories:	379	Fat:	15 g.
Protein:	23 g.	Cholesterol:	81 mg.
Carbohydrate:	38 g.	Sodium:	559 mg.

Kielbasa in Beer

1 pound packaged kielbasa, sliced on the diagonal
2 tablespoons chopped onion
1 clove garlic, minced
1 can (12 ounces) beer
1 can (16 ounces) sauerkraut

Makes 6 servings

Place kielbasa in 2-quart casserole. Cover. Microwave at HIGH (100%) 2 to 3 minutes. Stir; add onions and garlic. Microwave at HIGH (100%) 2 to 3 minutes. Add beer and sauerkraut.

Microwave at HIGH (100%) until heated through, 2 to 3 minutes. Drain before serving.

Per Serving:			
Calories:	247	Fat:	21 g.
Protein:	10 g.	Cholesterol:	51 mg.
Carbohydrate:	4 g.	Sodium:	985 mg.

Sweet and Sour Pork

2 tablespoons packed brown sugar
2 tablespoons cornstarch
1 can (8 ounces) pineapple chunks (juice pack), drained (reserve juice)
¼ cup teriyaki sauce
3 tablespoons cider vinegar
1½ teaspoons catsup
1 pound boneless pork shoulder or loin, cut into ¾-inch cubes
2 medium green peppers, cut into ¾-inch chunks

Makes 4 servings

Mix brown sugar and cornstarch in 2-quart casserole. Blend in pineapple juice, teriyaki sauce, vinegar and catsup. Stir in pork and peppers.

Cover. Microwave at HIGH (100%) 5 minutes. Stir in pineapple chunks. Cover. Microwave at MEDIUM (50%) until pork is cooked and sauce is thickened, 4 to 5 minutes, stirring once. Serve over rice, if desired.

Per Serving:			
Calories:	315	Fat:	13 g.
Protein:	23 g.	Cholesterol:	82 mg.
Carbohydrate:	26 g.	Sodium:	781 mg.

Herbed Pork Tenderloin

1½ pound pork tenderloin
1 tablespoon butter
2 cloves garlic, minced
1 teaspoon marjoram
½ teaspoon oregano
½ teaspoon pepper
2 tablespoons flour
1 envelope chicken bouillon
2 tablespoons water
2 tablespoons wine

Makes 6 servings

Place butter in 2-cup measure. Microwave at HIGH (100%) until melted, 20 to 30 seconds. Add garlic, marjoram, oregano and pepper. Mix well. Brush on tenderloin.

Place tenderloin in oven roasting bag and tie loosely. Slit bag 6 times near tie so juices will not run out during cooking. Place bag in pie dish.

Microwave at MEDIUM-LOW (30%) until meat is no longer pink, 13 to 17 minutes, turning bag and meat over halfway through cooking. Remove tenderloin to serving dish. Cover with foil and let stand 5 minutes.

Optional Gravy: Pour juice from bag into 2-cup measure and add remaining ingredients. Microwave at HIGH (100%) until thickened, 2 to 3 minutes, stirring 2 times during cooking. Slice tenderloin. Pour gravy over tenderloin and serve.

Per Serving:			
Calories:	162	Fat:	5 g.
Protein:	24 g.	Cholesterol:	79 mg.
Carbohydrate:	3 g.	Sodium:	397 mg.

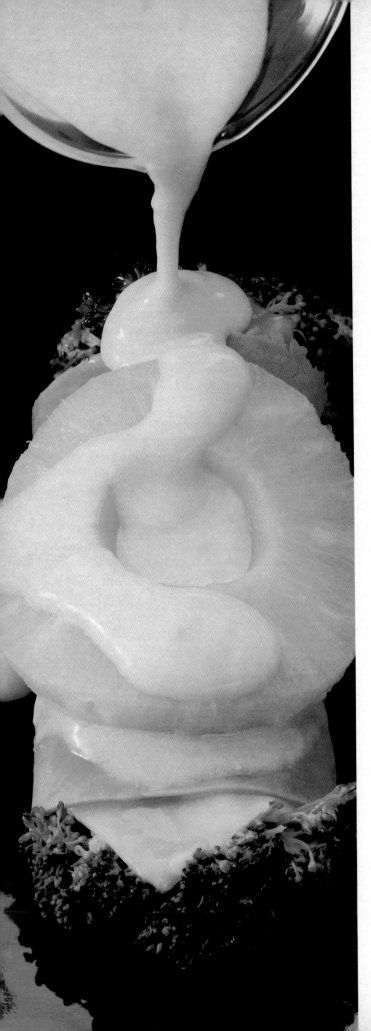

◄ Ham-Broccoli Rolls

1 package (10 ounces) frozen broccoli spears
1 tablespoon margarine or butter
2 tablespoons all-purpose flour
2 teaspoons prepared horseradish
2 teaspoons prepared mustard
½ teaspoon Worcestershire sauce
½ teaspoon instant minced onion
1 can (8 ounces) pineapple slices (juice pack), drained (reserve juice)
  Pineapple juice
½ cup milk
1 egg, slightly beaten
4 1-ounce slices Swiss cheese (⅛ inch thick)
4 1-ounce slices boiled ham

Makes 4 servings

Place broccoli spears in 1-quart casserole. Microwave at HIGH (100%) until tender, 5 to 7 minutes; drain. Set aside.

Place margarine in a medium bowl. Microwave at HIGH (100%) until melted, 30 to 45 seconds. Stir in flour, horseradish, mustard, Worcestershire sauce and instant onion. Add enough pineapple juice to reserved juice to measure 1 cup. Stir juice and milk into flour mixture. Blend in egg.

Microwave at MEDIUM-HIGH (70%) until thickened, 3 to 5 minutes, stirring twice.

Divide broccoli spears into 4 equal portions. Place a cheese slice on top of each ham slice. Place broccoli spears on top of cheese. Spoon 1 tablespoon sauce over each. Roll ham and cheese around broccoli; place seam side down in loaf dish, 9 × 5 inches.

Pour ¼ cup sauce over ham-broccoli rolls. Top with pineapple slices. Microwave at MEDIUM-HIGH (70%) until cheese is melted and sauce is bubbly, 3 to 5 minutes. Microwave remaining sauce at MEDIUM-HIGH (70%) until hot, 30 seconds to 1 minute. Stir. Serve over ham-broccoli rolls.

Per Serving:			
Calories:	304	Fat:	15 g.
Protein:	19 g.	Cholesterol:	112 mg.
Carbohydrate:	25 g.	Sodium:	537 mg.

Ham Loaf ▲

¾ pound ground ham
½ pound ground veal
¼ pound ground pork
2 eggs, beaten
1 cup soft bread crumbs
½ cup pineapple juice
¼ cup chopped onion
1 teaspoon prepared mustard
⅛ teaspoon pepper
¼ cup packed brown sugar
2 tablespoons pineapple juice
2 teaspoons prepared mustard

Makes 6 servings

Mix ham, veal and pork in medium bowl. Mix eggs, bread crumbs, ½ cup pineapple juice, onion, 1 teaspoon mustard and pepper. Stir into meat mixture. Shape into loaf in casserole or pie plate.

Mix brown sugar, 2 tablespoons pineapple juice and 2 teaspoons mustard. Spread over ham loaf. Microwave at MEDIUM-HIGH (70%) until internal temperature reaches 165°F., 20 to 25 minutes. Let stand covered with aluminum foil 5 to 10 minutes.

Per Serving:			
Calories:	308	Fat:	15 g.
Protein:	23 g.	Cholesterol:	148 mg.
Carbohydrate:	19 g.	Sodium:	884 mg.

Lamb Chops à l'Orange

4 lamb rib chops, about 1½ inches thick
¼ teaspoon garlic salt
½ cup orange marmalade
4 ¼-inch-thick orange slices

Makes 4 servings

Sprinkle both sides of lamb chops lightly with garlic salt. Place in 10-inch square casserole with meatiest portions toward outside of casserole. Spoon one-fourth of the marmalade on each lamb chop; top each with 1 orange slice. Cover.

Microwave at MEDIUM-HIGH (70%) until lamb chops are desired doneness, 11 to 13 minutes. Rearrange lamb chops once during cooking.

Per Serving:			
Calories:	233	Fat:	5 g.
Protein:	19 g.	Cholesterol:	65 mg.
Carbohydrate.	30 g.	Sodium:	167 mg.

◄ Leg of Lamb with Sherry-Herb Sauce

4 to 5-pound leg of lamb
2 cloves garlic, cut into thin slices
1 teaspoon dried tarragon leaves
1 teaspoon dried rosemary leaves
1 teaspoon margarine or butter
2 tablespoons margarine or butter
1 small clove garlic, minced
2 tablespoons flour
1 cup milk
2 tablespoons sherry
¼ teaspoon salt
½ teaspoon rosemary, crumbled

Makes 6 servings

Cut small slits in lamb roast. Place garlic slices in slits. Mix 1 teaspoon each tarragon, rosemary and margarine in small bowl. Microwave at HIGH (100%) until margarine is melted, 30 to 45 seconds. Brush over lamb roast. Place roast fat side down on roasting rack. Estimate total cooking time; divide in half. (See chart below.)

Microwave at MEDIUM (50%) first half of cooking time. Turn roast over. Microwave for second half of cooking time or until lamb reaches desired internal temperature. Let stand 10 minutes covered with aluminum foil.

While lamb roast is standing, place margarine and garlic in 4-cup measure. Microwave at HIGH (100%) until margarine is melted and garlic is softened, 1½ to 2 minutes. Blend in flour, milk, sherry, salt and rosemary. Microwave at HIGH (100%) until thickened and hot, 2 to 3 minutes, stirring after half the cooking time.

Doneness	Time/Pound	Internal Temperature
Rare	5-8 min./lb.	120°F.
Medium	7-10 min./lb.	135°F.
Well Done	9-12 min./lb.	150°F.

Per Serving:			
Calories:	397	Fat:	18 g.
Protein:	48 g.	Cholesterol:	151 mg.
Carbohydrate:	5 g.	Sodium:	274 mg.

Veal Continental ▲

    1 cup thinly sliced fresh mushrooms
    ½ cup chopped onion
    2 tablespoons margarine or butter
  1½ pounds boneless veal, cut into ¾- to 1-inch
      cubes
    1 cup water
    1 can (8 ounces) tomato sauce
    ¼ cup all-purpose flour
    2 teaspoons instant beef bouillon
    1 bay leaf
    ½ teaspoon salt
    ¼ teaspoon pepper
    1 medium tomato, cut into 8 wedges

Makes 4 servings

Combine mushrooms, onion and margarine in 2-quart casserole. Microwave at HIGH (100%) until onion is tender, 4 to 6 minutes. Stir in remaining ingredients except tomato wedges. Cover. Microwave at HIGH (100%) 5 minutes. Reduce power to MEDIUM-HIGH (70%). Microwave until veal is tender, 16 to 22 minutes, stirring after half the cooking time.

Stir in tomato wedges; cover. Microwave at MEDIUM-HIGH (70%) until tomatoes are tender, 5 to 7 minutes, stirring after half the cooking time. Serve over noodles or ricè, if desired.

Per Serving:			
Calories:	375	Fat:	20 g.
Protein:	35 g.	Cholesterol:	122 mg.
Carbohydrate:	14 g.	Sodium:	930 mg.

Veal Cordon Bleu

  1½ pounds (6 slices) veal scallopine
    ¼ teaspoon thyme
    ½ teaspoon salt
    ¼ teaspoon pepper
    6 slices (¼ pound) deli ham
    6 slices (¼ pound) Swiss cheese
    2 tablespoons butter
    1 medium onion, chopped
    2 tablespoons flour
    1 teaspoon or envelope instant chicken broth
    ½ cup water
    ½ cup white wine

Makes 6 servings

Pound veal and sprinkle with thyme, salt and pepper. Top each slice with 1 slice of ham and 1 slice of cheese. Roll tightly lengthwise and secure with toothpicks. Set aside.

Combine butter and onion in 3-quart casserole. Microwave at HIGH (100%) until tender, 2 to 3 minutes. Stir in flour and bouillon. Add water, wine and veal rolls. Cover.

Microwave at MEDIUM (50%) until veal is tender, 10 to 13 minutes, turning once during cooking.

Per Serving:			
Calories:	293	Fat:	13 g.
Protein:	34 g.	Cholesterol:	126 mg.
Carbohydrate:	6 g.	Sodium:	907 mg.

POULTRY

◄Roast Turkey

10-pound ready-to-cook turkey,
    giblets removed

Makes 10 to 12 servings

Place turkey breast side down on roasting rack or on saucer in rectangular baking dish, 12 × 8 inches, or 10-inch square casserole. Cover with vented plastic wrap. Calculate total cooking time, allowing 10 to 14 minutes per pound. Divide total time in half.

Microwave at MEDIUM (50%) first half of the total time. Turn turkey breast side up; baste. Shield turkey with aluminum foil as needed; re-cover.

Microwave last half of total time or until internal temperature reaches 170°F. when meat thermometer is inserted in meatiest part of breast and thigh on both sides of turkey. Let stand tented with aluminum foil 15 minutes.

Per Serving:			
Calories:	324	Fat:	9 g.
Protein:	56 g	Cholesterol:	145 mg.
Carbohydrate:	—	Sodium:	134 mg.

Dressing▲

8 ounces fresh mushrooms, sliced
½ cup chopped onion
½ cup chopped celery
½ cup margarine or butter
1 egg
1 package (8 ounces) seasoned stuffing mix
    (about 4 cups)
1 cup hot water
1½ teaspoons instant chicken bouillon
1 teaspoon ground sage

Makes 8 servings

Combine mushrooms, onion, celery and margarine in 2-quart casserole. Microwave at HIGH (100%) until vegetables are tender, 5 to 8 minutes.

Stir in remaining ingredients. Microwave at HIGH (100%) until heated through, 4 to 7 minutes, stirring once during cooking.

Per Serving:			
Calories:	230	Fat:	13 g.
Protein:	5 g.	Cholesterol:	36 mg.
Carbohydrate:	23 g.	Sodium:	598 mg.

Herb Roasted Chicken

3 tablespoons margarine or butter
2 cloves garlic, minced
3 tablespoons grated Parmesan cheese
1 tablespoon rosemary
½ teaspoon ground sage
¾ teaspoon thyme leaves
¾ teaspoon basil leaves
3 to 4-pound roasting chicken

Makes 6 servings

Place margarine in 2-cup measure or small bowl. Microwave at HIGH (100%) until soft, 10 to 20 seconds. Add garlic, cheese and spices. Mix until creamy.

Turn chicken breast side up and work the handle of a rubber scraper under the skin at the openings on each side of the breast. Continue into thigh and leg and make the skin as smooth as possible. Using the rubber scraper, spread herb mixture evenly under skin. Place chicken in 10-inch pie plate or casserole and cover with vented plastic wrap.

Microwave at MEDIUM-HIGH (70%) until internal temperature reaches 170°F. and chicken next to the bone is no longer pink, 5 to 8 minutes per pound, turning chicken over halfway through cooking time. Let stand loosely covered with aluminum foil 5 to 10 minutes.

Variation: Use herb mixture with turkey breast. Follow times on poultry chart, page 35.

Per Serving:			
Calories:	372	Fat:	25 g.
Protein:	34 g.	Cholesterol:	106 mg.
Carbohydrate:	1 g.	Sodium:	214 mg.

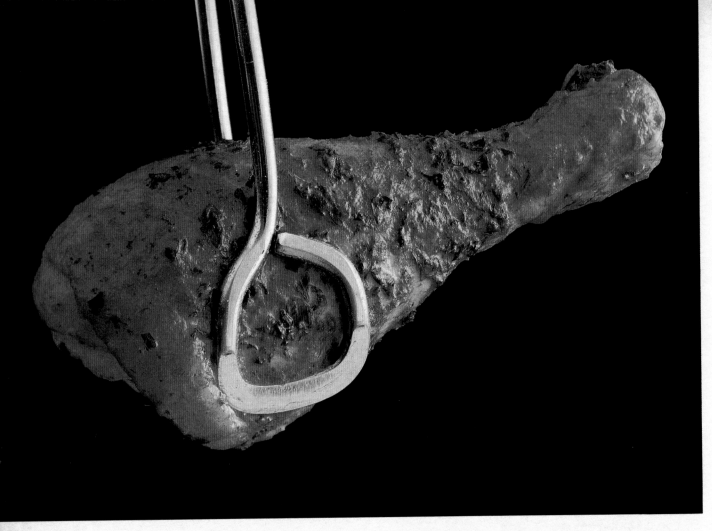

Seasoned Drumsticks ▲

1/4 cup margarine or butter
1 tablespoon dried parsley flakes
2 teaspoons chopped chives
1 teaspoon dried tarragon leaves
1/4 teaspoon salt
1/4 teaspoon pepper
8 chicken drumsticks

Makes 4 servings

Place margarine in small bowl. Microwave at HIGH (100%) until melted, 45 seconds to 1 minute 30 seconds. Stir in remaining ingredients except chicken. Set aside.

Place chicken drumsticks in rectangular baking dish, 12 X 8 inches, or 10-inch square casserole with meatiest portions to outside of dish. Brush with half of the margarine mixture. Microwave at MEDIUM-HIGH (70%) until chicken next to bone is not pink, 15 to 20 minutes, turning over, rearranging and brushing with remaining margarine mixture after half the cooking time.

Per Serving:			
Calories:	257	Fat:	16 g.
Protein:	25 g.	Cholesterol:	82 mg.
Carbohydrate:	1 g.	Sodium:	347 mg.

Honey Dijon Chicken

1 tablespoon margarine or butter, melted
3 tablespoons Dijon mustard
2 tablespoons lemon juice
1/2 cup honey
1/4 teaspoon salt
1/4 teaspoon white pepper
6 chicken breasts, boneless and skinless
2 tablespoons water
1 tablespoon cornstarch
1 tablespoon snipped fresh parsley

Makes 6 servings

In a 10-inch baking dish, mix first six ingredients. Microwave at HIGH (100%) 35 seconds. Add chicken. Marinate in refrigerator.

Cover with wax paper. Microwave at HIGH (100%) for 4 to 7 minutes. Turn chicken over. Microwave at MEDIUM-HIGH (70%) until chicken is not pink, 4 to 7 minutes. Place chicken on serving dish and cover. Mix water and cornstarch in 2-cup measure; add honey mustard sauce. Microwave at HIGH (100%) until thickened, 1 to 2 minutes. Pour over chicken and sprinkle with parsley.

Per Serving:			
Calories:	248	Fat:	4 g.
Protein:	27 g.	Cholesterol:	69 mg.
Carbohydrate:	26 g.	Sodium:	417 mg.

Chicken Breasts Parmesan

1 can (8 ounces) tomato sauce
1 teaspoon Italian seasoning
¼ teaspoon garlic salt
⅓ cup cornflake crumbs
¼ cup grated Parmesan cheese
1 teaspoon dried parsley flakes
2 large boneless chicken breasts (1½ to 2 pounds), split and skin removed
1 egg, beaten
½ cup shredded mozzarella cheese (about 2 ounces)
Grated Parmesan cheese

Makes 6 servings

Mix tomato sauce, Italian seasoning and garlic salt in 2-cup measure. Cover with wax paper. Microwave at HIGH (100%) 2 minutes. Stir. Reduce power to MEDIUM (50%). Microwave 5 minutes; stirring once. Set sauce aside.

Mix cornflake crumbs, ¼ cup Parmesan cheese and the parsley flakes. Dip chicken breasts in beaten egg, then in crumb mixture. Place in rectangular baking dish, 12 × 8 inches, or 10-inch square casserole. Cover with wax paper. Microwave at MEDIUM-HIGH (70%) until chicken is tender, 8 to 12 minutes, rearranging after half the cooking time. (Do not turn over.)

Pour sauce over chicken. Sprinkle mozzarella over chicken breasts. Sprinkle with Parmesan cheese. Microwave at MEDIUM-HIGH (70%) until mozzarella melts and sauce is hot, 2 to 4½ minutes.

Per Serving:			
Calories:	217	Fat:	7 g.
Protein:	30 g.	Cholesterol:	119 mg.
Carbohydrate:	8 g.	Sodium:	572 mg.

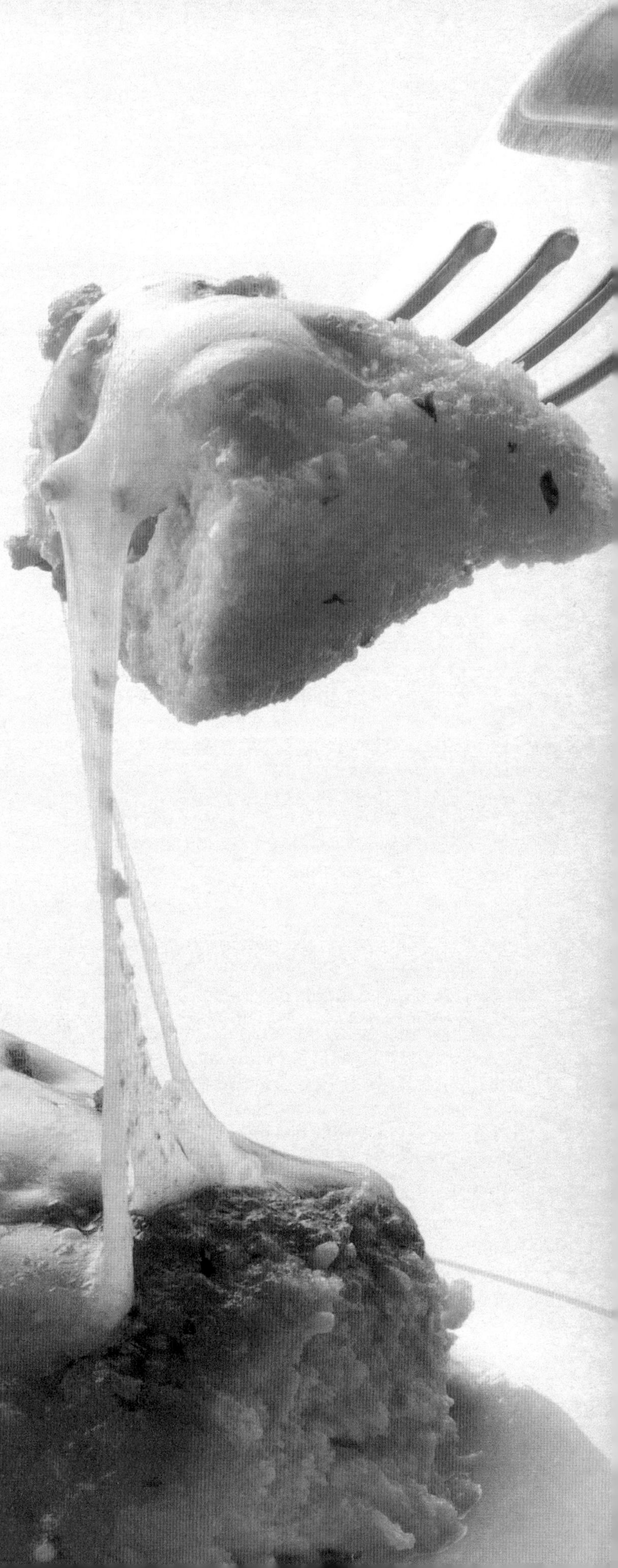

Brunswick Stew ▲

1 package (10 ounces) frozen whole kernel corn
1 package (10 ounces) frozen lima beans
1 package (10 ounces) frozen okra
2½ to 3-pound broiler-fryer chicken, cut up
2 cups hot water
1 medium onion, thinly sliced and separated into rings
½ teaspoon salt
¼ teaspoon pepper
⅛ teaspoon garlic powder
1 bay leaf
2 medium tomatoes, each cut into 8 wedges
¼ cup all-purpose flour

Makes 6 servings

Place corn, lima beans and okra in 2-quart casserole in oven. Microwave at HIGH (100%) until defrosted, 6 to 8 minutes. Drain. Cut okra into ½-inch pieces. Set aside.

Combine chicken, water, onion, salt, pepper, garlic powder and bay leaf in 3- to 5-quart casserole; cover. Microwave at HIGH (100%) until chicken next to bone is not pink, 18 to 25 minutes. Remove bay leaf. Remove bones and skin from chicken; cut meat into 1-inch pieces. Add chicken, tomatoes, flour, corn, lima beans and okra to chicken broth mixture.

Microwave, uncovered, at HIGH (100%) until stew is slightly thickened, 16 to 22 minutes, stirring after half the cooking time.

Per Serving:			
Calories:	261	Fat:	5 g.
Protein:	24 g.	Cholesterol:	54 mg.
Carbohydrate:	31 g.	Sodium:	261 mg.

Gourmet Chicken Salad

1 pound chicken breasts, boneless and skinless
1 Granny Smith apple, cut into chunks
3 slices bacon, cooked and crumbled
¾ cup coarsely chopped walnuts
½ cup mayonnaise
¼ teaspoon garlic salt
¼ teaspoon onion powder

Makes 4 servings

Place chicken breasts on roasting rack with meatiest portions to the outside of dish. Cover with vented plastic wrap. Microwave at HIGH (100%) until chicken is not pink, 4 to 7 minutes, turning halfway through cooking. Cool and dice into ½-inch chunks.

Combine remaining ingredients with chicken and chill until ready to serve. Serve as a salad on a bed of lettuce or in a sandwich.

Pasta Chicken Salad Variation: Add 2 cups cooked fusilli, rotini or cheese tortellini and increase mayonnaise to ¾ cup.

Other Variations: Use chopped scallions, grape halves, raisins or change walnuts to either cashews or toasted slivered almonds.

Per Serving:			
Calories:	520	Fat:	40 g.
Protein:	31 g.	Cholesterol:	86 mg.
Carbohydrate:	12 g.	Sodium:	421 mg.

Chicken and Shrimp in Red Wine Sauce ▶

¼ cup margarine or butter
1 medium onion, chopped
2 cloves garlic, minced
2½ to 3-pound broiler-fryer chicken, cut up, or boneless 1½-pounds chicken breast
1 can (8 ounces) tomato sauce
¾ cup rosé wine
¼ cup all-purpose flour
2 tablespoons snipped parsley
½ teaspoon salt
1 teaspoon dried basil leaves
½ teaspoon Italian seasoning
¼ teaspoon pepper
1 pound raw shrimp, shelled and deveined, fresh or frozen, defrosted

Makes 6 servings

Combine margarine, onion and garlic in 3- to 5-quart casserole. Microwave at HIGH (100%) until onion is tender-crisp, 3 to 5 minutes. Stir in remaining ingredients except shrimp.

Microwave at MEDIUM-HIGH (70%) until chicken next to bone is not pink, 22 to 28 minutes, turning and rearranging chicken pieces after half the cooking time. Remove chicken pieces and place in serving dish. Cover; set aside.

Add shrimp to wine sauce. Microwave at HIGH (100%) until shrimp turns pink (do not overcook or shrimp will become tough), 2 to 4 minutes, stirring after half the cooking time. Skim any fat from surface of sauce. Pour shrimp sauce over chicken pieces.

Per Serving:	
Calories:	327
Protein:	34 g.
Carbohydrate:	10 g.
Fat:	14 g.
Cholesterol:	169 mg.
Sodium:	663 mg.

Chicken Cacciatore

2 cups thinly sliced fresh mushrooms
½ cup chopped onion
1 clove garlic, minced
1 can (15 ounces) tomato sauce
1 can (6 ounces) tomato paste
½ cup water
½ cup red wine
1½ teaspoons dried oregano leaves
1½ teaspoons dried parsley flakes
1 teaspoon sugar
½ teaspoon salt
¼ teaspoon pepper
¼ teaspoon dried thyme leaves
2½ to 3-pound broiler-fryer chicken, cut up

Makes 4 servings

Combine mushrooms, onion and garlic in 3- to 5-quart casserole. Microwave at HIGH (100%) until tender, 4 to 6 minutes. Stir in remaining ingredients except chicken. Add chicken pieces, stirring to coat.

Microwave at MEDIUM-HIGH (70%) until chicken next to bone is not pink, 22 to 28 minutes, rearranging after half the cooking time.

Per Serving:					
Calories:	289	Carbohydrate:	22 g.	Cholesterol:	81 mg.
Protein:	31 g.	Fat:	8 g.	Sodium:	1328 mg.

Chicken Stroganoff ▾

3 tablespoons butter
1 small onion, finely chopped
1 clove garlic, minced
3 cups cooked cubed chicken
1 can (4 ounces) sliced mushrooms
¼ cup dry sherry
1 tablespoon cornstarch
½ teaspoon salt
1 cup sour cream
2 tablespoons chopped pimiento
    Puff pastry shells, rice or noodles

Makes 6 servings

Place butter, onion and garlic in 2-quart casserole. Microwave at HIGH (100%) until tender, 3 to 5 minutes. Add chicken and mushrooms. Dissolve cornstarch and salt in sherry. Stir into chicken onion mixture. Microwave at HIGH (100%) until thickened, 2 to 3 minutes. Stir in sour cream and pimiento. Microwave at MEDIUM-HIGH (70%) until hot, 2 to 4 minutes, stirring once during cooking. Serve over puff pastry shells, rice or noodles.

Per Serving:			
Calories:	298	Fat:	19 g.
Protein:	22 g.	Cholesterol:	95 mg.
Carbohydrate:	6 g.	Sodium:	399 mg.

Peanutty Curried Chicken

1 pound chicken breasts, boneless and skinless, cut into 1-inch cubes
⅓ cup flour
½ cup crunchy peanut butter
½ cup buttermilk
1 egg
1½ teaspoons curry powder
1 tablespoon lemon juice
½ teaspoon salt
¼ teaspoon cayenne pepper
1 cup seasoned bread crumbs
¼ cup margarine or butter, melted
1 cup prepared fruited chutney

Makes 4 servings

Roll chicken pieces in flour. Combine remaining ingredients except bread crumbs, margarine and chutney. Dip chicken in peanut butter mixture; roll in bread crumbs. Place chicken pieces in 8-inch round or square casserole. Drizzle with melted margarine.

Microwave at HIGH (100%) until chicken is tender, 8 to 11 minutes. Heat chutney and serve as a dipping sauce with chicken.

Per Serving:			
Calories:	796	Fat:	32 g.
Protein:	42 g.	Cholesterol:	120 mg.
Carbohydrate:	86 g.	Sodium:	2188 mg.

Chicken and Dumplings ▲

2½ to 3-pound broiler-fryer chicken, cut up
3 medium carrots, thinly sliced
2 cups hot water
6 peppercorns
2 bay leaves
½ teaspoon salt
¾ cup water
6 tablespoons all-purpose flour
½ teaspoon dried sage leaves
1 cup frozen peas, defrosted
1 can (4 ounces) sliced mushrooms, drained
1 cup buttermilk baking mix
1 tablespoon dried parsley flakes
⅓ cup milk

Makes 6 servings

Per Serving:			
Calories:	269	Fat:	8 g.
Protein:	22 g.	Cholesterol:	55 mg.
Carbohydrate:	27 g.	Sodium:	581 mg.

Place chicken, carrots, 2 cups water, the peppercorns, bay leaves and salt in 3- to 5-quart casserole; cover. Microwave at HIGH (100%) until chicken next to bone is not pink, 16 to 22 minutes, stirring after half the cooking time. Remove bones and skin from chicken; cut into small pieces. Return chicken meat to casserole. Remove bay leaves and peppercorns. Skim excess fat from chicken broth.

Blend ¾ cup water, the flour and sage until smooth. Stir into chicken mixture. Cover. Microwave at HIGH (100%) until slightly thickened, 13 to 16 minutes. Stir 2 or 3 times during cooking. Stir in peas and mushrooms.

Stir baking mix, parsley flakes and milk with fork just until moistened. Drop dough in 6 spoonfuls onto hot chicken mixture. Cover. Microwave at MEDIUM-HIGH (70%) until dumplings are set, 3½ to 5 minutes.

Turkey Divan

2 tablespoons margarine or butter
2 tablespoons all-purpose flour
⅓ cup hot water
1 to 2 teaspoons instant chicken bouillon
¼ cup whipping cream
2 tablespoons sherry
⅛ teaspoon nutmeg
¼ cup grated Parmesan cheese
1 pound sliced cooked turkey or chicken
1 package (10 ounces) frozen broccoli spears, defrosted
2 tablespoons grated Parmesan cheese
Dash of paprika

Makes 4 servings

Place margarine in medium bowl. Microwave at HIGH (100%) until melted, 30 seconds to 1 minute. Blend in flour. Stir in water, bouillon, cream, sherry and nutmeg. Microwave at MEDIUM-HIGH (70%) until thickened, 4 to 7 minutes, stirring 2 or 3 times. Stir in ¼ cup Parmesan. Set aside.

Place turkey slices in square baking dish, 8 × 8 inches. Arrange broccoli spears over top. Pour cream sauce over broccoli. Sprinkle with 2 tablespoons Parmesan cheese and the paprika. Microwave at MEDIUM-HIGH (70%) until heated through, 6 to 8 minutes.

Per Serving:			
Calories:	381	Fat:	20 g.
Protein:	40 g.	Cholesterol:	114 mg.
Carbohydrate:	8 g.	Sodium:	434 mg.

White Chili

2 large onions, chopped
1 tablespoon olive oil
3 cloves garlic, minced
1 can (4 ounces) mild green chilies, chopped
2 cans (19 ounces each) cannellini (white kidney) beans, drained
1 can (13¾ ounces) chicken broth
4 cups cut-up cooked chicken breasts
2 teaspoons ground cumin
1½ teaspoons oregano
½ teaspoon salt
¼ teaspoon cayenne pepper
3 cups grated Monterey Jack cheese
Salsa
Sour cream

Makes 8 servings

Turkey Rice Supreme

4 tablespoons margarine or butter
3 stalks celery, chopped
1 medium onion, chopped
1 can (10¾ ounces) cream of chicken soup
1 pound processed cheese spread, cut into chunks
½ cup milk
3 cups cooked cubed turkey
4 cups cooked rice
2 cans (8 ounces each) sliced water chestnuts

Makes 6 servings

Combine margarine, celery and onion in 4-cup measure or bowl. Microwave at HIGH (100%) until tender, 5 to 7 minutes.

Combine soup and cheese in 3-quart casserole. Microwave at HIGH (100%) until cheese is melted, 2 to 4 minutes, stirring once during heating. Add milk; stir well. Add celery mixture and remaining ingredients.

Microwave at MEDIUM-HIGH (70%) until heated through, 10 to 13 minutes, stirring once during cooking.

Per Serving:			
Calories:	688	Fat:	31 g.
Protein:	41 g.	Cholesterol:	115 mg.
Carbohydrate:	63 g.	Sodium:	1725 mg.

Combine onions, oil and garlic in 5-quart measure. Cover. Microwave at HIGH (100%) until tender, 5 to 7 minutes. Stir.

Add all remaining ingredients except cheese, salsa and sour cream. Mix well and cover. Microwave at HIGH (100%) until boiling, 8 to 10 minutes. Stir well. Microwave at MEDIUM (50%) 45 to 55 minutes, stirring several times during cooking. Serve topped with cheese, salsa and sour cream.

Per Serving:			
Calories:	423	Fat:	19 g.
Protein:	41 g.	Cholesterol:	99 mg.
Carbohydrate:	22 g.	Sodium:	957 mg.

◄ Shrimp Scampi

¼ cup margarine or butter
1 large clove garlic, minced
2 tablespoons lemon juice
1 pound jumbo raw shrimp, shelled and deveined
2 tablespoons minced fresh parsley
Paprika

Makes 4 servings

Place margarine and garlic in 10-inch round glass dish or pie plate. Microwave at HIGH (100%) until margarine is melted and garlic begins to soften, 1½ to 2½ minutes. Stir in lemon juice. Add shrimp and toss to coat. Cover with vented plastic wrap.

Microwave at MEDIUM-HIGH (70%) until shrimp are pink, opaque and tender (do not overcook or shrimp will become tough), 3½ to 6 minutes, stirring twice. Sprinkle with parsley and paprika.

Per Serving:			
Calories:	203	Fat:	13 g.
Protein:	19 g.	Cholesterol:	140 mg.
Carbohydrate:	2 g.	Sodium:	272 mg.

Oriental Fish

½ cup water
¼ cup soy sauce
¼ cup dry sherry
2 tablespoons packed brown sugar
½ teaspoon ground ginger
⅛ teaspoon garlic powder
16 ounces fish fillets, fresh or frozen, defrosted

Makes 4 servings

Combine all ingredients except fish in square baking dish, 8 X 8 inches. Stir until blended. Add fish, coating both sides. Cover; refrigerate 1 hour.

Place fish fillets on roasting rack. Microwave at MEDIUM-HIGH (70%) until fish flakes easily in center with fork, 5 to 7 minutes.

Per Serving:			
Calories:	133	Fat:	1 g.
Protein:	22 g.	Cholesterol:	54 mg.
Carbohydrate:	5 g.	Sodium:	629 mg.

Fillet of Flounder with Broccoli

1 package (10 ounces) frozen chopped broccoli
¼ cup margarine or butter
¼ cup all-purpose flour
1 teaspoon dried tarragon leaves
½ teaspoon salt
⅛ teaspoon pepper
¼ teaspoon paprika
1 cup milk
¼ cup dry white wine
1 tablespoon lemon juice
12 ounces flounder fillets, fresh or frozen, defrosted

Makes 4 servings

Place frozen broccoli in 1-quart casserole; cover. Microwave at HIGH (100%) until broccoli is tender, 5 to 7 minutes. Drain. Set aside. Place margarine in medium bowl. Microwave at HIGH (100%) until melted, 45 seconds to 1 minute 30 seconds. Blend in flour, tarragon, salt, pepper and paprika. Gradually stir in milk, wine and lemon juice. Microwave at MEDIUM-HIGH (70%) until thickened, 4 to 6 minutes, stirring once or twice. Set sauce aside.

Place fish in rectangular baking dish, 12 X 8 inches, or 10-inch square casserole. Cover with wax paper. Microwave at HIGH (100%) until fish flakes easily in center with fork, 5 to 7 minutes. Drain and remove fish fillets.

Spread reserved broccoli in baking dish. Arrange fish fillets over top. Pour reserved sauce over fish and broccoli. Microwave at MEDIUM-HIGH (70%) until heated through, 1½ to 3 minutes.

Per Serving:			
Calories:	271	Fat:	14 g.
Protein:	21 g.	Cholesterol:	45 mg.
Carbohydrate:	14 g.	Sodium:	516 mg.

Salmon-Stuffed Sole ▲

¼ cup chopped onion
¼ cup chopped celery
2 tablespoons margarine or butter
1 can (7¾ ounces) salmon, drained and
    bones removed
3 tablespoons dry bread crumbs
1 teaspoon grated lemon peel
⅛ teaspoon pepper
2 fresh sole fillets (8 ounces each)
⅛ teaspoon paprika
2 tablespoons margarine or butter
1½ tablespoons all-purpose flour
¼ teaspoon salt
⅛ teaspoon pepper
⅛ teaspoon paprika
¾ cup half-and-half or milk
¼ cup white wine

Makes 4 servings

Place onion, celery and 2 tablespoons margarine in medium bowl. Microwave at HIGH (100%) until tender, 2 to 4 minutes. Stir in salmon, crumbs, lemon peel and pepper.

Place 1 fillet on roasting rack. Top with stuffing and remaining fillet. Sprinkle with ⅛ teaspoon paprika. Cover with wax paper. Microwave at HIGH (100%) until fish flakes easily, 5 to 7 minutes. Let stand, covered.

Place 2 tablespoons margarine in medium bowl. Microwave at HIGH (100%) until melted, 30 seconds to 1 minute. Stir in flour, salt, ⅛ teaspoon pepper and paprika. Blend in half-and-half and wine. Microwave at HIGH (100%) until thickened, 2 to 4 minutes, stirring once.

Per Serving:			
Calories:	380	Fat:	22 g.
Protein:	33 g.	Cholesterol:	91 mg.
Carbohydrate:	10 g.	Sodium:	652 mg.

Trout Almondine

¼ cup margarine or butter
½ cup slivered almonds
2 teaspoons almond liqueur
2 packages (10 ounces each) frozen whole pan-
    dressed trout, defrosted or 4 fresh pan-dressed
    trout (5 ounces each)

Makes 4 servings

Per Serving:			
Calories:	404	Fat:	28 g.
Protein:	32 g.	Cholesterol:	82 mg.
Carbohydrate:	5 g.	Sodium:	209 mg.

Place margarine in 1-quart casserole or small bowl. Microwave at HIGH (100%) until melted, 45 seconds to 1 minute 30 seconds. Stir in almonds and liqueur. Microwave at HIGH (100%) until almonds are light brown, 3 to 3½ minutes, stirring after every minute. Remove almonds with a slotted spoon. Set almonds and margarine aside.

Arrange trout in rectangular baking dish, 12 X 8 inches, or 10-inch square casserole. Pour reserved margarine over trout. Cover with wax paper. Microwave at MEDIUM-HIGH (70%) until fish flakes easily in center with a fork, 5 to 9 minutes, turning over and rearranging after half the time. Sprinkle with almonds.

Fillet of Sole in Lemon Parsley Butter

½ cup margarine or butter
2 tablespoons all-purpose flour
2 tablespoons fresh lemon juice
1 tablespoon snipped parsley
¼ teaspoon salt
⅛ teaspoon pepper
⅛ teaspoon celery seed
1 pound sole or flounder fillets, fresh or frozen, defrosted

Makes 4 servings

Place margarine in rectangular baking dish, 12 × 8 inches, or 10-inch square casserole. Microwave at HIGH (100%) until melted, 45 seconds to 1 minute 30 seconds. Blend in remaining ingredients except fish fillets.

Coat both sides of fish fillets with butter sauce. Arrange in the baking dish. Cover with wax paper. Microwave at MEDIUM-HIGH (70%) until fish flakes easily in center with fork, 5 to 7 minutes.

Per Serving:			
Calories:	324	Fat:	24 g.
Protein:	22 g.	Cholesterol:	54 mg.
Carbohydrate:	4 g.	Sodium:	494 mg.

◄ Crab Imperial

    4 tablespoons margarine or butter
    4 tablespoons finely chopped celery
    3 tablespoons finely chopped scallions
    1 tablespoon each finely chopped
        red and green pepper
    1 teaspoon dry mustard
    ½ teaspoon salt
    3 tablespoons flour
    1 cup milk
    ¼ cup sherry
    1 tablespoon lemon juice
    3 tablespoons mayonnaise
    2 cans (8 ounces each) crabmeat,
        drained and cartilage removed

Makes 4 servings

Place margarine, celery, scallions and peppers in 1½-quart casserole. Cover and microwave at HIGH (100%) until vegetables are tender, 2 to 3 minutes. Add mustard, salt and flour, stirring until smooth. Gradually add milk, sherry and lemon juice, stirring well. Microwave, uncovered, at HIGH (100%) until thickened and bubbly, 3 to 5 minutes, stirring after 2 minutes. Stir in mayonnaise and crabmeat. Microwave at HIGH (100%) until heated through, 2 to 4 minutes. Serve over puff pastry shells or rice, if desired.

Per Serving:			
Calories:	350	Fat:	23 g.
Protein:	21 g.	Cholesterol:	92 mg.
Carbohydrate:	11 g.	Sodium:	796 mg.

Poached Fish

    16 ounces fish fillets, fresh or frozen, defrosted
    ½ cup dry white wine
    ¼ teaspoon salt
    ⅛ teaspoon pepper

Makes 4 servings

Place fish fillets in square baking dish, 8 × 8 inches. Pour wine over fish fillets. Sprinkle with salt and pepper.

Cover with plastic wrap. Microwave at MEDIUM-HIGH (70%) until fish flakes easily in center with fork, 5 to 7 minutes.

Per Serving:			
Calories:	123	Fat:	1 g.
Protein:	21 g.	Cholesterol:	54 mg.
Carbohydrate:	1 g.	Sodium:	228 mg.

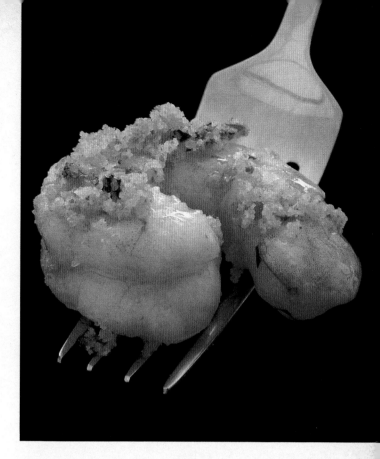

Shrimp de Jonghe ▲

    ½ cup margarine or butter, cut into 4 pieces
    4 cloves garlic, sliced
    ½ cup sherry
    1 tablespoon snipped parsley
    ½ teaspoon salt
    1 teaspoon chopped chives
    ¼ teaspoon dried tarragon leaves
    ¼ teaspoon instant minced onion
        Dash of ground nutmeg
        Dash of dried thyme leaves
    ¾ cup dry bread crumbs
    2 pounds raw shrimp, shelled and deveined

Makes 6 servings

Combine margarine and garlic in 1½-quart casserole. Microwave at HIGH (100%) until garlic is browned, 4 to 5 minutes. Remove and discard garlic. Stir in sherry, parsley, salt, chives, tarragon, instant onion, nutmeg and thyme. Remove ¼ cup of seasoned margarine; stir into bread crumbs.

Mix shrimp into remaining margarine in casserole until coated. Microwave at MEDIUM-HIGH (70%) 5 minutes. Stir. Sprinkle with bread crumbs. Microwave at MEDIUM-HIGH (70%) until shrimp is pink and opaque, 1 to 4 minutes. Let stand 2 minutes.

Per Serving:			
Calories:	335	Fat:	18 g.
Protein:	25 g.	Cholesterol:	173 mg.
Carbohydrate:	13 g.	Sodium:	617 mg.

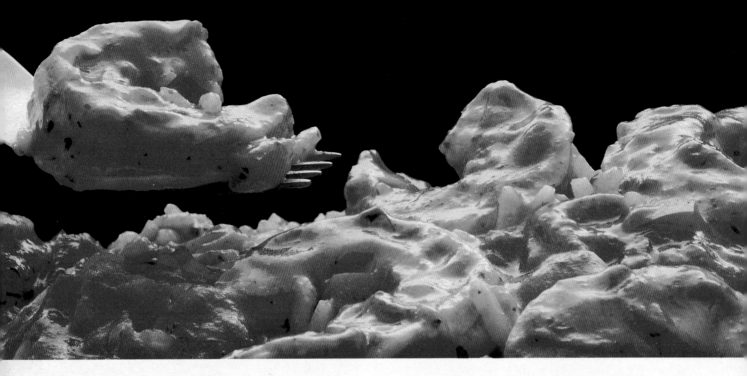

Shrimp Creole ▲

1 medium onion, chopped
¾ cup chopped green pepper
¼ cup chopped celery
3 tablespoons margarine or butter
1 can (16 ounces) whole tomatoes
1 can (6 ounces) tomato paste
1 cup water
2 tablespoons all-purpose flour
2 tablespoons dried parsley flakes
1½ teaspoons sugar
½ teaspoon salt
½ teaspoon chili powder
⅛ teaspoon pepper
⅛ teaspoon dried thyme leaves
⅛ teaspoon red pepper sauce
12 ounces raw shrimp, shelled and deveined

Makes 4 servings

Combine onion, green pepper, celery and margarine in 3-quart casserole. Microwave at HIGH (100%) until vegetables are tender, 3 to 6 minutes. Add tomatoes, tomato paste, water and flour, stirring to break up tomatoes. Mix in remaining ingredients except shrimp. Cover.

Microwave at HIGH (100%) until mixture is bubbly, 8 to 10 minutes, stirring twice during cooking. Stir in shrimp; cover. Microwave at HIGH (100%) until shrimp is opaque and tender (do not overcook or shrimp will become tough), 3½ to 5 minutes, stirring once or twice during cooking. Let stand 2 minutes. Serve with rice, if desired.

Per Serving:			
Calories:	241	Fat:	11 g.
Protein:	17 g.	Cholesterol:	97 mg.
Carbohydrate:	22 g.	Sodium:	997 mg.

Coquilles St. Jacques

1 tablespoon margarine or butter
1 tablespoon chopped onion
1 pound scallops
1 cup sliced fresh mushrooms
⅓ cup white wine
1½ teaspoons lemon juice
¼ teaspoon salt
  Dash of dried marjoram leaves
  Dash of paprika
3 tablespoons margarine or butter
2 tablespoons all-purpose flour
½ cup whipping cream or half-and-half
1 tablespoon snipped parsley

Makes 4 servings

Combine 1 tablespoon margarine and onion in 1½-quart casserole. Microwave at HIGH (100%) 1 minute. Stir in scallops, mushrooms, wine, lemon juice, salt, marjoram and paprika. Microwave, covered, at HIGH (100%) 3 minutes. Drain and reserve liquid.

Place 3 tablespoons margarine in small bowl. Microwave at HIGH (100%) until melted, 30 seconds to 1 minute. Blend in flour. Stir in ½ cup reserved scallop liquid, cream and parsley. Microwave at MEDIUM-HIGH (70%) until thickened, 2½ to 4 minutes, stirring once. Stir sauce into scallops.

Spoon scallop mixture into 4 ramekins or small bowls. Microwave at MEDIUM-HIGH (70%) until heated through, 1½ to 3 minutes. (Do not overcook.)

Per Serving:			
Calories:	342	Fat:	23 g.
Protein:	21 g.	Cholesterol:	78 mg.
Carbohydrate:	9 g.	Sodium:	464 mg.

Scalloped Oysters

2 tablespoons margarine or butter
½ cup dry bread crumbs
¼ teaspoon paprika
¼ cup chopped celery
1 tablespoon margarine or butter
1 pint shucked oysters, drained
1 can (10½ ounces) condensed cream of chicken
    soup
¼ cup dry bread crumbs
2 tablespoons half-and-half or milk
1 tablespoon dried parsley flakes
¼ teaspoon salt
⅛ teaspoon pepper

Makes 4 servings

Place 2 tablespoons margarine in small bowl. Microwave at HIGH (100%) until melted, 30 seconds to 1 minute. Stir in ½ cup bread crumbs and the paprika. Set aside.

Place celery and 1 tablespoon margarine in 1-quart casserole. Microwave at HIGH (100%) until celery is tender, 2 to 4 minutes. Add oysters; cover. Microwave at HIGH (100%) until edges of oysters are curled, 3 to 4 minutes. Stir in soup, ¼ cup bread crumbs, the half-and-half, parsley, salt and pepper.

Microwave at HIGH (100%) until hot and bubbly, 5 to 7 minutes, stirring after half the cooking time. Sprinkle with buttered bread crumbs during last 2 minutes of cooking time.

Per Serving:
Calories:	307	Fat:	17 g.
Protein:	13 g.	Cholesterol:	70 mg.
Carbohydrate:	25 g.	Sodium:	1084 mg.

Steamed Clams ▾

2 pounds shell clams (cherrystone or littleneck)
½ cup water

Makes 6 servings

Per Serving:
Calories:	63	Fat:	1 g.
Protein:	11 g.	Cholesterol:	29 mg.
Carbohydrate:	2 g.	Sodium:	48 mg.

Wash shells of clams thoroughly, discarding any broken or open clams. Set aside.

Pour water into 2-quart casserole; cover. Microwave at HIGH (100%) until water boils, 3 to 4 minutes. Add clams; cover. Microwave at HIGH (100%) until clams open, 4 to 6 minutes, stirring after half the cooking time.

EGGS, CHEESE & SAUCES

This section includes favorite egg and cheese dishes that are as great for a late-day supper as they are for breakfast. You'll learn how easy it is to turn out smooth, memorable sauces without worrying about scorching, sticking or overcooking.

Scrambled Eggs

Eggs	Butter	Milk	Time
1	1 tbsp.	1 tbsp.	1½-2 min.
2	1 tbsp.	2 tbsp.	1¼-1¾ min.
4	1 tbsp.	2 tbsp.	2-3 min.
6	2 tbsp.	¼ cup	3¼-4¼ min.

Place butter in casserole or serving dish. Microwave at HIGH (100%) until butter melts, about 45 seconds. Add eggs and milk and scramble with a fork. Following the chart, microwave at HIGH (100%) half the time.

Eggs will start to set around edge of dish. Break up cooked portions with fork; stir them to center of dish. Microwave remaining time, stirring once or twice more from outside to center.

Stop cooking while eggs still look moist, soft and slightly underdone. If cooked until they are as firm as you like, they will be overcooked and tough when served. Let stand 1 to 4 minutes; stir again. If not firm enough, microwave a few seconds more.

Per Serving:			
Calories:	189	Fat:	17 g.
Protein:	7 g.	Cholesterol:	276 mg.
Carbohydrate:	1 g.	Sodium:	211 mg.

Poached Eggs

½ cup hot tap water
1 teaspoon white vinegar
4 eggs

Makes 4 servings

Place 2 tablespoons water and ¼ teaspoon vinegar in each of four 6-ounce custard cups. Arrange in oven in a circle. Microwave at HIGH (100%) until water boils, 1½ minutes.

Break 1 egg into each custard cup. Prick yolk. Cover each loosely with plastic wrap. Reduce power to MEDIUM-HIGH (70%). Microwave until egg whites are opaque and egg yolks are soft-set, 1½ to 2 minutes.

Per Serving:			
Calories:	79	Fat:	6 g.
Protein:	6 g.	Cholesterol:	275 mg.
Carbohydrate:	1 g.	Sodium:	69 mg.

Puffy Omelet ▲

1 tablespoon margarine or butter
4 eggs or egg substitute
¼ cup milk or half-and-half
¼ teaspoon baking powder
¼ teaspoon salt
  Dash of pepper

Makes 4 servings

Place margarine in 9-inch pie plate. Microwave at HIGH (100%) until melted, 45 seconds. Separate eggs, placing egg whites in large mixing bowl and egg yolks in medium bowl. Blend remaining ingredients into egg yolks. Beat whites with electric mixer until stiff but not dry.

Fold egg yolk mixture into beaten egg whites with rubber spatula. Pour into pie plate. Microwave at MEDIUM (50%) until center is set, 5 to 6 minutes.

Cheese Omelet Variation: Sprinkle ½ cup shredded cheese over cooked omelet. Microwave at MEDIUM-HIGH (70%) until cheese melts, 30 seconds to 1 minute.

Western Omelet Variation: Combine ½ cup chopped onion, ½ cup chopped green pepper and 1 tablespoon olive oil in medium bowl or 4-cup measure. Microwave at HIGH (100%) until vegetables are tender, 2½ to 3 minutes. Stir in 1 cup diced fully cooked ham. Sprinkle over omelet during last minute of cooking time. If necessary, microwave an additional 30 seconds to 1 minute.

Per Serving:			
Calories:	113	Fat:	9 g.
Protein:	7 g.	Cholesterol:	276 mg.
Carbohydrate:	1 g.	Sodium:	276 mg.

Cheese Fondue ▲

 1 clove garlic, cut in half
 4 cups shredded Swiss cheese (about 16 ounces)
¼ cup all-purpose flour
¼ teaspoon salt
¼ teaspoon ground nutmeg
⅛ teaspoon pepper
1½ cups white wine
   French bread, cut into 1-inch cubes

Makes 6 servings

Rub inside of 2-quart casserole with garlic. Discard garlic. Combine cheese, flour, salt, nutmeg and pepper in plastic bag. Shake to coat cheese. Set aside.

Pour wine into 2-quart casserole. Microwave at MEDIUM-HIGH (70%) until wine is very hot but not boiling, 2 to 4 minutes. Add all ingredients from plastic bag. Blend with wire whisk.

Microwave at MEDIUM-HIGH (70%) until bubbly, 4 to 6 minutes. Stir with wire whisk until smooth. Serve with bread cubes.

Per Serving:			
Calories:	354	Fat:	21 g.
Protein:	22 g.	Cholesterol:	70 mg.
Carbohydrate:	9 g.	Sodium:	288 mg.

Macaroni and Cheese

 3 tablespoons margarine or butter
 2 tablespoons all-purpose flour
¼ teaspoon salt
½ teaspoon dry mustard
¼ teaspoon pepper
 4 drops red pepper sauce
1½ cups milk
 2 cups shredded Cheddar cheese or
   1 cup each shredded Cheddar and
   Swiss cheese (about 8 ounces)
12 ounces elbow macaroni, cooked and drained
 3 tablespoons margarine or butter
½ cup seasoned dry bread crumbs

Makes 6 servings

Place 3 tablespoons margarine in 2-quart casserole. Microwave at HIGH (100%) until melted, 30 seconds to 1 minute. Blend in flour, salt, mustard, pepper and red pepper sauce. Stir in milk.

Microwave at HIGH (100%) until thickened, 4 to 6 minutes, blending with wire whisk once or twice during cooking. Stir in cheese. Microwave at HIGH (100%) to soften cheese, 30 seconds to 1 minute 30 seconds. Stir in macaroni.

Place 3 tablespoons margarine in small bowl. Microwave at HIGH (100%) until melted, 30 seconds to 1 minute. Stir in bread crumbs; sprinkle over casserole. Microwave at MEDIUM-HIGH (70%) until heated through, 5 to 7 minutes.

Per Serving:			
Calories:	549	Fat:	27 g.
Protein:	20 g.	Cholesterol:	48 mg.
Carbohydrate:	55 g.	Sodium:	759 mg.

Sauces

Medium White Sauce ▶

2 tablespoons margarine or butter
2 tablespoons all-purpose flour
¼ teaspoon salt
1 cup milk

Makes 6 servings

Place margarine in 1-quart casserole. Microwave at HIGH (100%) until melted, 30 seconds to 1 minute. Stir in flour and salt. Blend in milk.

Microwave at HIGH (100%) until thickened, 3 to 6 minutes, stirring once or twice during cooking.

Cheese Sauce Variation: Stir ¾ cup shredded Cheddar cheese and a dash of cayenne pepper into cooked white sauce. Microwave at HIGH (100%) to melt cheese, 30 seconds to 1 minute.

Per Serving:			
Calories:	64	Fat:	5 g.
Protein:	2 g.	Cholesterol:	3 mg.
Carbohydrate:	4 g.	Sodium:	154 mg.

Hollandaise Sauce

3 egg yolks
1 tablespoon lemon juice
¼ teaspoon salt
  Dash of cayenne pepper (optional)
½ cup margarine or butter

Makes 4 servings

Blend egg yolks, lemon juice, salt and cayenne pepper in small bowl. Set aside. Place margarine in another small bowl. Microwave at HIGH (100%) just until melted, 30 to 40 seconds, stirring once or twice.

Blend egg yolk mixture into margarine with wire whisk. Microwave at MEDIUM-LOW (30%) until thickened, 1 to 1½ minutes, blending with wire whisk every 15 seconds. Check sauce often when it begins to thicken. Blend with wire whisk before serving.

Per Serving:			
Calories:	252	Fat:	27 g.
Protein:	2 g.	Cholesterol:	204 mg.
Carbohydrate:	1 g.	Sodium:	408 mg.

Mornay Sauce ▲

2 tablespoons margarine or butter
2 tablespoons all-purpose flour
1 cup chicken stock or broth
¼ cup half-and-half or milk
¼ cup grated Romano cheese
¼ cup shredded Swiss cheese (about 1 ounce)
2 teaspoons chopped fresh parsley

Makes 8 servings

Place margarine in 4-cup measure. Microwave at HIGH (100%) until melted, 30 seconds to 1 minute. Stir in flour. Blend in chicken stock or broth and half-and-half.

Microwave at MEDIUM-HIGH (70%) until thickened and smooth, 4 to 6 minutes, stirring 2 or 3 times. Stir in Romano and Swiss cheese and parsley. Microwave at MEDIUM-HIGH (70%) 1 minute. Stir until cheese melts.

Per Serving:			
Calories:	73	Fat:	6 g.
Protein:	3 g.	Cholesterol:	9 mg.
Carbohydrate:	2 g.	Sodium:	181 mg.

SOUPS & BEVERAGES

Quickly cook satisfying soups in your Sharp Microwave Oven that taste like they've simmered all day. Try Irish coffee, hot buttered rum or cocoa for a late-night warm-up.

◄ Confetti Soup

3 tablespoons butter or margarine
1 cup cubed carrots, ¼-inch cubes
1 cup cubed rutabaga, ¼-inch cubes
½ cup chopped onion
½ cup chopped celery
1 cup fresh broccoli flowerets or cauliflowerets
¼ cup all-purpose flour
½ teaspoon salt
½ teaspoon pepper
¼ teaspoon sugar
4 cups milk
1 cup shredded pasteurized process American cheese
1 cup frozen corn
½ cup cubed fully cooked ham, ¼-inch cubes
½ cup frozen peas

Makes 6 servings

Combine butter, carrots, rutabaga, onion, celery and broccoli in 3-quart casserole. Cover. Microwave at HIGH (100%) until vegetables are tender, 9 to 14 minutes, stirring 3 times. Stir in flour, salt, pepper and sugar. Blend in milk. Reduce power to MEDIUM-HIGH (70%). Microwave, uncovered, until mixture is slightly thickened, 15 to 18 minutes, stirring after every 4 minutes. Stir in cheese, corn, ham and peas. Microwave at MEDIUM-HIGH (70%) until heated through and cheese melts, 3 to 5 minutes, stirring once.

Per Serving:			
Calories:	302	Fat:	16 g.
Protein:	15 g.	Cholesterol:	36 mg.
Carbohydrate:	27 g.	Sodium:	786 mg.

Split Pea Soup

1 can (13¾ ounces) beef broth
4 cups water
1 pound dried green split peas (about 2 cups), soaked overnight and drained
3 medium carrots, coarsely grated
1 medium onion, chopped
½ teaspoon salt
¼ teaspoon pepper
⅛ teaspoon thyme
½ pound ham, diced

Makes 8 servings

Combine all ingredients in 5-quart casserole; cover. Microwave at HIGH (100%) 10 minutes.

Reduce power to MEDIUM (50%). Microwave until vegetables are tender and soup is slightly thickened, 40 to 50 minutes, stirring 2 or 3 times during cooking. Puree half of the soup in blender. Return to remaining soup in casserole. Stir and serve.

Per Serving:			
Calories:	269	Fat:	4 g.
Protein:	20 g.	Cholesterol:	16 mg.
Carbohydrate:	40 g.	Sodium:	804 mg.

New England Clam Chowder

3 slices bacon, chopped
2 cans (6½ ounces each) minced clams, drained (reserve ⅓ cup liquid)
1½ cups cubed potatoes, ½-inch cubes
½ cup chopped onion
3 tablespoons all-purpose flour
1½ cups milk
⅛ teaspoon pepper
1 cup half-and-half or milk

Makes 4 servings

Place bacon in 2-quart casserole. Microwave at HIGH (100%) until bacon is crisp, 3 to 4 minutes. Add reserved clam juice, potatoes and onion. Cover. Microwave at HIGH (100%) until potatoes are tender, 8 to 10 minutes, stirring after half the cooking time.

Blend in flour. Stir in milk and pepper. Microwave at HIGH (100%) until thickened, 5 to 7 minutes, stirring twice during cooking time.

Blend in half-and-half; stir in clams. Microwave at MEDIUM-HIGH (70%) until thickened and heated through, 4 to 5 minutes.

Per Serving:			
Calories:	297	Fat:	12 g.
Protein:	21 g.	Cholesterol:	66 mg.
Carbohydrate:	26 g.	Sodium:	282 mg.

Vegetable Soup

1 clove garlic, minced
1 cup chopped celery
1 cup chopped onion
2 cups cubed potatoes, ½-inch cubes
1 cup thinly sliced carrots
1 cup water
1 tablespoon all-purpose flour
1 can (10½ ounces) beef consommé
1 can (14 ounces) whole tomatoes with liquid,
   chopped
1 package (10 ounces) frozen green peas
¼ teaspoon pepper

Makes 8 servings

Combine garlic, celery and onion in 5-quart casserole. Microwave at HIGH (100%) until vegetables are tender, 2 to 3 minutes.

Add potatoes, carrots and water; cover. Microwave at HIGH (100%) until potatoes are tender, 12 to 14 minutes, stirring after half the cooking time.

Blend flour into consommé. Stir flour, consommé, tomatoes, green peas and pepper into vegetable mixture. Cover. Microwave at HIGH (100%) until soup is slightly thickened and peas are heated through, 8 to 10 minutes, stirring after half the cooking time.

Per Serving:			
Calories:	96	Fat:	1 g.
Protein:	5 g.	Cholesterol:	–
Carbohydrate:	19 g.	Sodium:	335 mg.

Autumn Soup ▲

1 pound lean ground beef
1 cup chopped onion
1 cup chopped celery
4 cups hot water
2 cups cubed potatoes, ½-inch cubes
1 cup thinly sliced carrots
½ teaspoon salt
½ teaspoon dried basil leaves
¼ teaspoon pepper
1 bay leaf
3 tomatoes, cut into eighths and sliced in half

Makes 8 servings

Mix ground beef, onion and celery in 5-quart casserole. Microwave at HIGH (100%) until ground beef loses its pink color, 5 to 7 minutes, stirring after half the cooking time.

Add hot water, potatoes, carrots, salt, basil, pepper and bay leaf; cover. Microwave at HIGH (100%) until potatoes are tender, 18 to 20 minutes.

Add tomatoes. Microwave at HIGH (100%) until tomatoes are tender, 8 to 10 minutes. Remove and discard bay leaf.

Per Serving:			
Calories:	141	Fat:	5 g.
Protein:	13 g.	Cholesterol:	38 mg.
Carbohydrate:	12 g.	Sodium:	184 mg.

French Onion Soup

3 tablespoons margarine or butter
3 medium onions, thinly sliced
1½ cups water
1 can (13¾ ounces) beef broth
½ cup white wine
1 teaspoon Worcestershire sauce
½ teaspoon salt
4 ½-inch slices toasted French bread
1 cup grated Swiss cheese
¼ cup grated fresh Parmesan cheese

Makes 4 servings

Combine margarine and onion in 3-quart casserole. Microwave at HIGH (100%) until onions are tender-crisp, 6 to 8 minutes.

Add water, broth, wine, Worcestershire sauce and salt; cover. Microwave at HIGH (100%) 5 minutes. Reduce power to MEDIUM (50%). Microwave until onions are tender and flavors are blended, 10 to 15 minutes.

Ladle soup into 4 individual serving bowls. Place toast on top. Sprinkle each with ¼ cup Swiss cheese and 1 tablespoon Parmesan cheese. Microwave at HIGH (100%) until cheese softens, 1 to 2 minutes.

Per Serving:			
Calories:	357	Fat:	19 g.
Protein:	15 g.	Cholesterol:	31 mg.
Carbohydrate:	26 g.	Sodium:	1282 mg.

Canadian Cheese Soup ▲

1 can (13¾ ounces) chicken broth
1 large potato, shredded
1 medium onion, chopped
1 medium carrot, grated
1 stalk celery, finely chopped
½ cup half-and-half or milk
1½ cups shredded sharp Cheddar cheese
　　(about 6 ounces)

Makes 4 servings

Combine 1 cup broth, potato, onion, carrot and celery in 3-quart casserole; cover. Microwave at HIGH (100%) until potatoes are tender, 10 to 12 minutes, stirring after half the cooking time.

Stir in remaining broth and half-and-half; cover. Microwave at MEDIUM-HIGH (70%) until heated through, 4 to 6 minutes. Mix in cheese, stirring until melted.

Per Serving:			
Calories:	284	Fat:	19 g.
Protein:	14 g.	Cholesterol:	58 mg.
Carbohydrate:	15 g.	Sodium:	862 mg.

Quick Corn Chowder

3 slices bacon, chopped
¼ cup finely chopped onion
1½ tablespoons all-purpose flour
1 package (10 ounces) frozen whole kernel corn
1½ cups milk
1½ teaspoons snipped parsley
¼ teaspoon pepper

Makes 4 servings

Combine bacon and onion in 2-quart casserole. Microwave at HIGH (100%) until bacon is crisp and onion is tender, 4 to 6 minutes, stirring after half the cooking time. Drain.

Blend in flour. Stir in corn, milk, parsley and pepper. Microwave at HIGH (100%) until slightly thickened and corn is tender, 5 to 7 minutes, stirring twice during cooking time.

Per Serving:			
Calories:	228	Fat:	13 g.
Protein:	7 g.	Cholesterol:	24 mg.
Carbohydrate:	22 g.	Sodium:	164 mg.

Irish Coffee ▶

¾ to 1 cup strong black coffee
1½ ounces Irish whiskey
1 teaspoon sugar
1 tablespoon whipped cream

Makes 1 serving

Mix coffee, whiskey and sugar in large mug or cup. Microwave at HIGH (100%) until hot, 1½ to 2 minutes. Top with whipped cream.

Per Serving:			
Calories:	147	Fat:	3 g.
Protein:	–	Cholesterol:	10 mg.
Carbohydrate:	4 g.	Sodium:	5 mg.

Hot Cocoa for One

1 to 2 tablespoons sugar
2 teaspoons cocoa
2 tablespoons cold water
¾ cup milk

Makes 1 serving

Mix sugar, cocoa and cold water in large mug or cup. Microwave at HIGH (100%) until thickened, 20 to 40 seconds.

Blend in milk. Microwave at HIGH (100%) until hot, 1 to 2 minutes, stirring once or twice.

Per Serving:			
Calories:	193	Fat:	7 g.
Protein:	7 g.	Cholesterol:	26 mg.
Carbohydrate:	29 g.	Sodium:	90 mg.

Hot Buttered Rum

⅔ cup apple cider
1 tablespoon packed brown sugar
1 1-inch stick cinnamon
1½ ounces rum
1 teaspoon butter
Dash of ground nutmeg

Makes 1 serving

Stir cider and brown sugar in large mug or cup. Add cinnamon stick.

Microwave at HIGH (100%) until cider boils, 2 to 2½ minutes. Stir in rum. Top with butter and ground nutmeg.

Per Serving:			
Calories:	267	Fat:	4 g.
Protein:	–	Cholesterol:	10 mg.
Carbohydrate:	33 g.	Sodium:	49 mg.

Hot Spiced Cider

2 quarts apple cider
1 cup brown sugar
1 teaspoon whole cloves
1 teaspoon whole allspice
4 cinnamon sticks
1 quart unsweetened pineapple juice
1 lemon, sliced thin

Makes 3 quarts

In a 4-quart measure combine all ingredients except lemon slices. Stir well. Microwave at MEDIUM-HIGH (70%) 15 to 20 minutes, or until hot. Strain into serving container; garnish with lemon slices. Serve hot.

Per Serving:			
Calories:	98	Fat:	1 g.
Protein:	1 g.	Cholesterol:	–
Carbohydrate:	25 g.	Sodium:	6 mg.

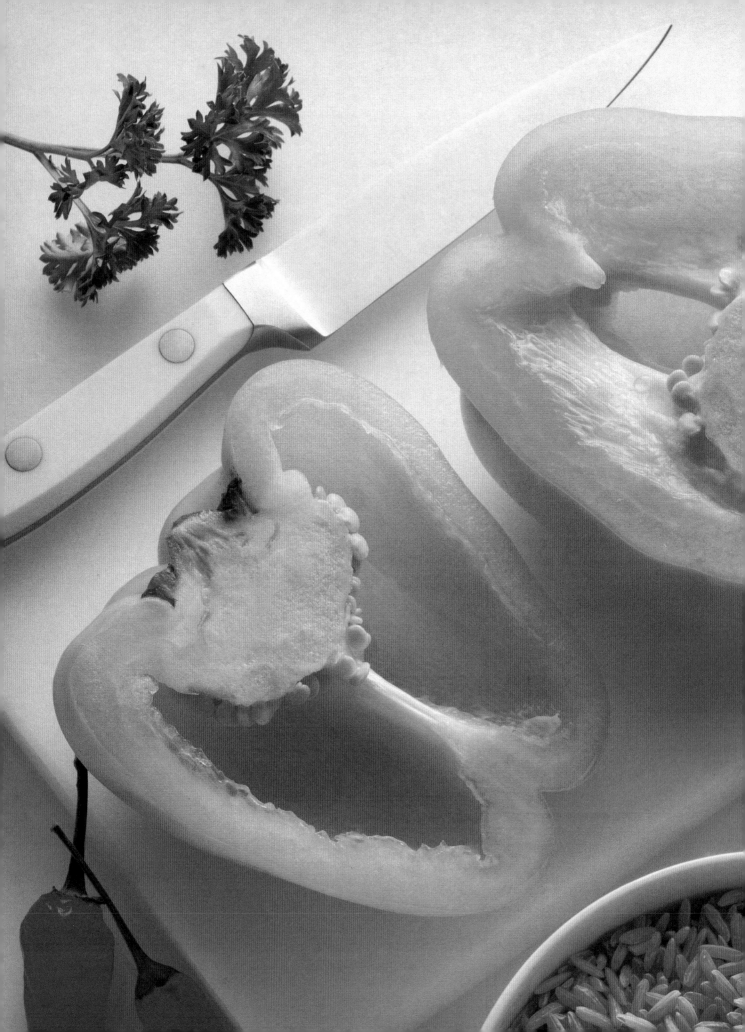

VEGETABLES

Fresh in color, texture and flavor, vegetables are naturals for microwave cooking. Vegetables cook quickly in a minimum of liquid, so they retain more vitamins and minerals.

Vegetable Chart

Vegetable	Amount	Cooking Procedure	Microwave Time at HIGH (100%)	Standing Time, Covered
Artichokes				
Fresh	2 medium	Trim and rinse. 2-qt. casserole. 2 tbsp. water. Cover with plastic wrap.	5-8 min.	5 min.
Asparagus				
Fresh Spears	1 lb.	2-qt. casserole. 2 tbsp. water. Cover. Rearrange after 3 min.	4-7 min.	2 min.
Frozen Spears	10-oz. pkg.	1-qt. casserole. 1 tbsp. water. Cover. Rearrange after 3 min.	7-9 min.	2 min.
Beans				
Fresh, Green and Wax	1 lb.	1½-in. pieces. 2-qt. casserole. ¼ cup water. Cover. Stir twice.	9-13 min.	2 min.
Frozen, Green	10-oz. pkg.	1-qt. casserole. 1 tbsp. water. Cover. Stir after 3 min.	5-7 min.	2 min.
Frozen, Lima	10-oz. pkg.	1-qt. casserole. 1 tbsp. water. Cover. Stir once.	6-9 min.	2 min.
Beets				
Fresh, Whole	5 medium	Wash. Leave 1 inch of tops. 2-qt. casserole. ¼ cup water. Cover. Stir every 5 min.	12-18 min.	3 min.
Broccoli				
Fresh, Spears	1 lb.	Wash. 2-qt. casserole. Add no water. Cover. Rearrange after 3 min. Uncover during stand.	6-8 min.	3 min., **uncovered**
Fresh, Pieces	1 lb.	Wash. 2-qt. casserole. Add no water. Cover. Stir after 3 min. Uncover during stand.	5-7 min.	2 min., **uncovered**
Frozen, Spears, Cuts, Chopped	10-oz. pkg.	1-qt. casserole. 2 tbsp. water. Cover. Stir after 3 min. Uncover during stand.	5-7 min.	2 min., **uncovered**
Brussels Sprouts				
Fresh	4 cups	2-qt. casserole. ¼ cup water. Cover. Stir after 2 min.	6-8 min.	3 min.
Frozen	10-oz. pkg.	1-qt. casserole. 2 tbsp. water. Cover. Stir after 3 min.	6-8 min.	3 min.
Cabbage				
Shredded	1 lb.	2-qt. casserole. 2 tbsp. water. Cover. Stir after 4 min.	8-12 min.	2 min.
Wedges	1 lb.	2-qt. casserole. 2 tbsp. water. Cover. Rearrange after 5 min.	12-14 min.	3 min.
Carrots				
Fresh, Slices	2 cups	1-qt. casserole. 2 tbsp. water. Cover. Stir after 3 min.	5-8 min.	3 min.
Frozen, Slices	2 cups	1-qt. casserole. 1 tbsp. water. Cover. Stir after 3 min.	5-7 min.	3 min.
Cauliflower				
Fresh, Flowerets	2 cups	1-qt. casserole. 1 tbsp. water. Cover. Stir after 2 min.	3-5 min.	2 min.
Fresh, Whole	1½ lbs.	Remove leaves and core center. 2-qt. casserole. 2 tbsp. water. Cover.	7-9 min.	3 min.
Frozen, Flowerets	10-oz. pkg.	1-qt. casserole. 1 tbsp. water. Cover. Stir after 3 min.	4-6 min.	2 min.

Vegetable Chart

Vegetable	Amount	Cooking Procedure	Microwave Time at HIGH (100%)	Standing Time, Covered
Corn				
Fresh, on Cob	2 ears	9-in. pie plate. 2 tbsp. water. Cover. Rearrange after 4 min.	6-9 min.	5 min.
	4 ears	2-qt. oval or rectangular casserole. ¼ cup water. Cover.	12-14 min.	5 min.
Frozen, on Cob	2 ears	9-in. pie plate. 2 tbsp. water. Cover. Rearrange after 4 min.	6-8 min.	5 min.
	4 ears	2-qt. oval or rectangular casserole. ¼ cup water. Cover.	10-12 min.	5 min.
Frozen, Whole Kernel	10-oz. pkg.	1-qt. casserole. 1 tbsp. water. Cover. Stir after 2 min.	4-6 min.	2 min.
Okra				
Fresh, Whole	¾ lb.	1½-2-qt. casserole. ¼ cup water. Cover. Stir after 3 min.	8-10 min.	3 min.
Frozen, Whole or Slices	10-oz. pkg.	1½-2-qt. casserole. 2 tbsp. water. Cover. Stir after 3 min.	6-8 min.	3 min.
Peas, Black-Eyed				
Frozen	10-oz. pkg.	2-qt. casserole. ¼ cup water. Cover. Stir after 4 min.	8-10 min.	3 min.
Peas, Green				
Fresh	2 cups	1-qt. casserole. ¼ cup water. Cover. Stir after 3 min.	4-6 min.	3 min.
Frozen	10-oz. pkg.	1-qt. casserole. 1 tbsp. water. Cover. Stir after 3 min.	6-8 min.	3 min.
Potatoes				
Baked	2 medium	Prick; place on paper towels.	7-9 min.	5-10 min.
	4 medium	Turn over, rearrange at ½ time. Let stand, foil wrapped.	13-16 min.	5-10 min.
Boiled	4 medium	Peel and quarter potatoes. 2-qt. casserole. Cover. Stir after 5 min.	9-12 min.	3 min.
Spinach				
Fresh	1 lb.	Wash and trim. Add no water. 3-qt. casserole. Cover. Stir after 3 min.	5-7 min.	2 min.
Frozen, Leaf or Chopped	10-oz. pkg.	1-qt. casserole. Add no water. Cover. Stir after 3 min.	6-8 min.	2 min.
Squash				
Fresh, Acorn	1 whole	Prick; place on paper towel. Turn over after 4 min.	7-10 min.	5 min.
Fresh, Sliced Zucchini	2 cups	1-qt. casserole. Add no water. Cover. Stir after 2 min.	2-4 min.	1 min.
Frozen, Mashed	10-oz. pkg.	1-qt. casserole. Add no water. Cover. Break apart and stir after 3 min.	6-8 min.	2 min.
Sweet Potatoes				
Baked	2 medium	Prick; place on paper towels.	5-9 min.	5 min.
	4 medium	Turn over, rearrange after 5 min.	10-13 min.	5 min.
Tomatoes				
Fresh	2 medium	Halve tomatoes. Round dish.	2-4 min.	2 min.
	4 medium	Cover. Rearrange once.	5-8 min.	2 min.
Canned Vegetables	15-16 oz.	1-qt. casserole. Drain all but 2 tbsp. liquid. Stir once.	2-4 min.	2 min.

Zesty Squash ▲

¼ cup margarine or butter
1 clove garlic, minced
1 teaspoon dried oregano leaves
½ teaspoon dried basil leaves
¼ teaspoon salt
⅛ teaspoon pepper
2 medium zucchini, thinly sliced
1 medium yellow summer squash, thinly sliced
1 large tomato, cut into 8 wedges

Makes 4 servings

Place margarine and garlic in 2-quart casserole. Microwave at HIGH (100%) until margarine is melted, 1 to 1½ minutes. Mix in oregano, basil, salt and pepper. Add remaining ingredients except tomato. Toss to coat. Cover.

Microwave at HIGH (100%) until squash is tender, 5 to 10 minutes, stirring after half the cooking time. Stir in tomato. Cover; let stand 2 minutes.

Per Serving:			
Calories:	126	Fat:	12 g.
Protein:	2 g.	Cholesterol:	—
Carbohydrate:	5 g.	Sodium:	273 mg.

Wilted Spinach Salad

1 pound fresh spinach
6 slices bacon, chopped
3 tablespoons chopped onion
⅓ cup vinegar
⅓ cup water
2 tablespoons sugar
¼ teaspoon pepper

Makes 4 servings

Wash spinach. Remove thick stems and bruised leaves. Drain well and set aside in salad bowl.

Place bacon pieces in 1-quart casserole. Microwave at HIGH (100%) until bacon is crisp, 6 to 8 minutes, stirring after half the cooking time. Remove bacon and set aside on paper toweling.

Add onion to bacon fat. Microwave at HIGH (100%) until tender, 1½ to 2½ minutes. Add vinegar, water, sugar and pepper. Microwave on HIGH (100%) until boiling, 3 to 6 minutes. Immediately pour over spinach. Add bacon and toss well. Serve immediately.

Per Serving:			
Calories:	109	Fat:	5 g.
Protein:	6 g.	Cholesterol:	8 mg.
Carbohydrate:	12 g.	Sodium:	241 mg.

Italian Zucchini ▶

4 medium zucchini (about 1½ pounds), thinly
   sliced
1 tablespoon margarine or butter
1 tablespoon olive oil
2 teaspoons snipped parsley
½ teaspoon dried basil leaves
½ teaspoon dried oregano leaves
¼ teaspoon salt

Makes 6 servings

Place zucchini in 1½-quart casserole; cover. Microwave at HIGH (100%) until tender-crisp, 4 to 6 minutes. Drain.

Stir in remaining ingredients. Microwave at HIGH
(100%) until vegetables are tender, 2 to 4 minutes, stirring after half the cooking time.

Per Serving:			
Calories:	50	Fat:	4 g.
Protein:	1 g.	Cholesterol:	—
Carbohydrate:	3 g.	Sodium:	109 mg.

Ratatouille

1 medium eggplant (1 to 1½ pounds), peeled and
   cut into 1-inch cubes
1 medium onion, thinly sliced and separated into
   rings
1 green pepper, thinly sliced
1 large clove garlic, minced
¼ cup olive oil
1 medium zucchini (½ to ¾ pound), thinly sliced
1½ teaspoons dried basil leaves
1½ teaspoons dried marjoram leaves
½ teaspoon salt
¼ teaspoon pepper
1 large tomato, chopped

Makes 8 servings

Mix eggplant, onion, green pepper, garlic and olive oil
in 3-quart casserole. Microwave, covered, at HIGH
(100%) until onion and green pepper are tender, 8 to
10 minutes, stirring once or twice during cooking time.

Add zucchini, basil, marjoram, salt and pepper. Microwave, covered, at HIGH (100%) until eggplant and zucchini are tender, 5 to 7 minutes. Gently stir in tomato.
Let stand 5 minutes.

Per Serving:			
Calories:	86	Fat:	7 g.
Protein:	1 g.	Cholesterol:	—
Carbohydrate:	6 g.	Sodium:	138 mg.

Creamy Spinach ▲

2 packages (10 ounces each) frozen chopped
   spinach
1 tablespoon margarine or butter
2 tablespoons chopped onion
1 tablespoon flour
½ cup half-and-half or milk
½ teaspoon sugar
¼ teaspoon salt
¼ teaspoon pepper
⅛ teaspoon ground nutmeg

Makes 6 servings

Place spinach in a 2-quart casserole and cover. Microwave at HIGH (100%) until completely defrosted, 8 to
10 minutes. Drain and set aside.

Combine margarine and onions in 2-cup measure or
bowl. Microwave at HIGH (100%) until tender, 1 to 2
minutes. Stir in flour and add remaining ingredients.
Mix well. Microwave at MEDIUM-HIGH (70%) until
thick, 2 to 3 minutes, stirring every 30 seconds. Blend
in spinach.

Microwave at MEDIUM-HIGH (70%) until heated
through, 2 to 3 minutes, stirring once. Stir before serving.

Per Serving:			
Calories:	73	Fat:	5 g.
Protein:	4 g.	Cholesterol:	8 mg.
Carbohydrate:	6 g.	Sodium:	191 mg.

Cauliflower Scramble

2 packages (10 ounces each) cauliflower in cheese
  sauce
1 medium zucchini, thinly sliced
¼ cup chopped onion
2 tablespoons margarine or butter
2 medium tomatoes, each cut into 8 wedges
¼ teaspoon dried thyme leaves

Makes 6 servings

Remove cauliflower pouches from boxes. Place both
pouches in oven. Microwave at HIGH (100%) until defrosted but not hot, 4 to 6 minutes, rearranging pouches
once. Set aside.

Combine zucchini, onion and margarine in 2-quart
casserole. Microwave at HIGH (100%) until vegetables
are tender-crisp, 2½ to 4 minutes. Stir in cauliflower,
tomatoes and thyme. Microwave, covered, at HIGH
(100%) until heated through, 4½ to 6½ minutes. Stir
before serving.

Per Serving:			
Calories:	98	Fat:	5 g.
Protein:	2 g.	Cholesterol:	—
Carbohydrate:	11 g.	Sodium:	425 mg.

Herbed Carrots

4 cups (1 pound) carrots, sliced on the diagonal
4 tablespoons margarine or butter
1 teaspoon salt
2 tablespoons water
1 teaspoon sugar
½ teaspoon marjoram
2 tablespoons chopped fresh parsley

Makes 6 servings

Combine carrots, margarine, salt and water in 3-quart casserole and cover. Microwave at HIGH (100%) until tender, 9 to 11 minutes, stirring halfway through. Toss in remaining ingredients. Serve immediately.

Per Serving:			
Calories:	103	Fat:	8 g.
Protein:	1 g.	Cholesterol:	–
Carbohydrate:	8 g.	Sodium:	483 mg.

Fresh Cauliflower au Gratin

1 medium head cauliflower (about 1 pound), separated into flowerets
1 tablespoon water
1 tablespoon margarine or butter
1 tablespoon all-purpose flour
½ cup milk
1 tablespoon prepared mustard (optional)
½ teaspoon salt
1 cup shredded Cheddar cheese (about 4 ounces)
⅛ teaspoon paprika

Makes 4 servings

Place cauliflowerets and water in 2-quart casserole; cover. Microwave at HIGH (100%) until tender, 5 to 7 minutes, stirring after half the cooking time. Drain and set aside.

Place margarine in 2-cup measure. Microwave at HIGH (100%) until melted, 30 seconds to 1 minute. Stir in flour. Blend in milk, mustard and salt. Reduce power to MEDIUM-HIGH (70%). Microwave until thickened, 2 to 3 minutes, stirring every minute. Stir in cheese until melted. Pour over cauliflowerets; sprinkle with paprika.

Per Serving:			
Calories:	176	Fat:	13 g.
Protein:	9 g.	Cholesterol:	34 mg.
Carbohydrate:	6 g.	Sodium:	504 mg.

Orange Carrots ▲

4 large carrots (1 pound), cut in thin slices
¼ cup margarine or butter
1 tablespoon grated orange rind
1 teaspoon sugar

Makes 6 servings

Combine all ingredients in 1-quart casserole.

Cover. Microwave at HIGH (100%) until carrots are tender, 4 to 8 minutes, stirring after half the cooking time.

Per Serving:			
Calories:	103	Fat:	8 g.
Protein:	1 g.	Cholesterol:	–
Carbohydrate:	9 g.	Sodium:	116 mg.

◄ Artichokes with Mustard Sauce

4 medium artichokes
¼ cup water
½ cup prepared brown mustard
¼ cup mayonnaise or salad dressing
1 tablespoon horseradish sauce (optional)

Makes 4 servings

Slice 1 inch from top of artichokes; trim stem even with base. Cut off sharp tips of outer leaves. Rinse artichokes under cold water. Arrange in upright position in square baking dish, 8 × 8 inches. Pour ¼ cup water into baking dish. Cover with plastic wrap.

Microwave at HIGH (100%) until lower leaves can be pulled off with a slight tug and base is fork-tender, 8 to 14 minutes, rearranging artichokes once during cooking. Mix remaining ingredients. Serve with artichokes.

Per Serving:
Calories:	260	Fat:	14 g.
Protein:	9 g.	Cholesterol:	8 mg.
Carbohydrate:	33 g.	Sodium:	670 mg.

Broccoli in Lemon Sauce

2 packages (10 ounces each) frozen broccoli spears
2 tablespoons water
2 tablespoons margarine or butter
1 tablespoon all-purpose flour
½ cup milk
2 teaspoons grated lemon rind
⅛ teaspoon salt

Makes 6 servings

Place broccoli and water in 2-quart casserole; cover. Microwave at HIGH (100%) until heated through, 7 to 10 minutes, stirring to break apart after half the time. Drain and set aside.

Place margarine in small bowl or 2-cup measure. Microwave at HIGH (100%) until melted, 30 seconds to 1 minute. Stir in flour. Blend in remaining ingredients. Reduce power to MEDIUM-HIGH (70%). Microwave until thickened, 2½ to 3 minutes, stirring every 30 seconds to 1 minute. Pour over broccoli. Microwave at MEDIUM-HIGH (70%) until heated through, 1½ to 2½ minutes.

Per Serving:
Calories:	72	Fat:	4 g.
Protein:	3 g.	Cholesterol:	2 mg.
Carbohydrate:	7 g.	Sodium:	119 mg.

Sunshine Brussels Sprouts ▶

2 packages (10 ounces each) frozen Brussels
    sprouts
2 tablespoons water
¼ cup chopped onion
1 tablespoon margarine or butter
¼ cup half-and-half or milk
2 egg yolks, slightly beaten
1 tablespoon fresh lemon juice
⅛ teaspoon salt
    Dash of pepper

Makes 6 servings

Place Brussels sprouts and water in 2-quart casserole;
cover. Microwave at HIGH (100%) until tender, 6 to
8 minutes, stirring after half the cooking time. Drain
and set aside.

Place onion and margarine in 2-cup measure. Microwave at HIGH (100%) until onion is tender, 1 to 2 minutes. Blend in remaining ingredients. Reduce power to
MEDIUM-HIGH (70%). Microwave until thickened,
1½ to 2 minutes, stirring every 30 seconds. Pour over
Brussels sprouts. Microwave at MEDIUM-HIGH (70%)
until heated through, 1 minute.

Per Serving:			
Calories:	93	Fat:	5 g.
Protein:	5 g.	Cholesterol:	95 mg.
Carbohydrate:	9 g.	Sodium:	83 mg.

Chilled Asparagus Vinaigrette

1 pound fresh asparagus, trimmed
2 teaspoons water
½ cup olive oil
¼ cup red wine vinegar
1 teaspoon sugar
¼ teaspoon salt
¼ teaspoon pepper
2 tablespoons Dijon mustard
3 tablespoons chopped fresh parsley

Makes 4 servings

Place asparagus spears and water in 2-quart casserole
and cover with plastic wrap. Microwave at HIGH
(100%) until tender crisp, 4 to 7 minutes. Drain and
set aside.

Whisk together the remaining ingredients in a 2-cup
measure or bowl. Pour over warm asparagus. Chill
several hours to marinate before serving.

Variation: Substitute broccoli, cauliflower, yellow
squash or zucchini for asparagus. Check Vegetable
Chart on pages 86 and 87 for cooking time.

Per Serving:			
Calories:	268	Fat:	28 g.
Protein:	2 g.	Cholesterol:	–
Carbohydrate:	5 g.	Sodium:	362 mg.

Parsley Potatoes

6 medium red potatoes (about 2½ pounds),
   peeled and quartered
¼ cup water
¼ cup margarine or butter
1 tablespoon dried parsley flakes
¼ teaspoon salt
⅛ teaspoon pepper

Makes 6 servings

Place potatoes and water in 2-quart casserole; cover. Microwave at HIGH (100%) until fork-tender, 10 to 15 minutes, stirring after half the time. Let stand 5 minutes. Drain and set aside.

Place margarine in 2-cup measure. Microwave at HIGH (100%) 1 to 1½ minutes. Stir in remaining ingredients. Pour over potatoes. Toss to coat.

Per Serving:			
Calories:	187	Fat:	8 g.
Protein:	3 g.	Cholesterol:	—
Carbohydrate:	27 g.	Sodium:	188 mg.

Stuffed Baked Potatoes

4 baking potatoes (about 6 to 8 ounces each)
½ cup sour cream
2 tablespoons milk
¼ cup shredded Monterey Jack cheese
   (about 1 ounce)
2 tablespoons margarine or butter
2 teaspoons dried parsley flakes
½ teaspoon salt
¼ teaspoon pepper
¼ teaspoon dry mustard
¼ cup scallions, chopped
¼ cup shredded Cheddar cheese (about 1 ounce)
⅛ teaspoon paprika
1 teaspoon chives

Makes 4 servings

Bake potatoes. Cut thin slice from the top of each potato. Scoop out inside with a spoon, leaving a thin shell. Add remaining ingredients except ¼ cup cheese, paprika and chives to potatoes. Mash.

Spoon one-fourth of the potato mixture into each shell. Place stuffed potatoes on a microwave-safe dish. Sprinkle with remaining cheese, chives and paprika. Microwave at MEDIUM-HIGH (70%) until potatoes are heated through, 2½ to 4½ minutes.

Per Serving:			
Calories:	320	Fat:	17 g.
Protein:	8 g.	Cholesterol:	27 mg.
Carbohydrate:	36 g.	Sodium:	453 mg.

German Potato Salad ▲

6 slices bacon, chopped
½ cup chopped green onions
¼ cup white vinegar
2 tablespoons sugar
¼ teaspoon salt
6 medium potatoes (about 2½ pounds), peeled
   and cut into ¼-inch slices
¼ cup water

Makes 6 servings

Place bacon and green onions in small bowl or 1-quart casserole; cover. Microwave at HIGH (100%) until bacon is light brown, 5 to 7 minutes. Stir in vinegar, sugar and salt. Set aside.

Place potato slices and water in 2-quart casserole; cover. Microwave at HIGH (100%) until potatoes are fork-tender, 10 to 15 minutes, stirring after half the cooking time. Drain. Pour bacon and vinegar mixture over potato slices. Toss to coat.

Per Serving:			
Calories:	174	Fat:	3 g.
Protein:	5 g.	Cholesterol:	5 mg.
Carbohydrate:	32 g.	Sodium:	199 mg.

Green Beans Almondine ▲

1½ pounds fresh green beans
½ cup hot water
¼ teaspoon salt
⅓ cup slivered almonds
3 tablespoons margarine or butter
¼ teaspoon ground nutmeg (optional)
¼ teaspoon pepper

Makes 6 servings

Wash beans and break off ends. Break beans into 1- to 1½-inch pieces. Place in 2-quart casserole. Stir water and salt until salt is dissolved. Stir into beans. Cover.

Microwave at HIGH (100%) until beans are tender-crisp, 10 to 13 minutes, stirring once. Let stand 2 to 3 minutes. Drain.

Mix in almonds, margarine, nutmeg and pepper until margarine is melted. Microwave at HIGH (100%) until heated through, 1 minute.

Per Serving:			
Calories:	124	Fat:	9 g.
Protein:	3 g.	Cholesterol:	—
Carbohydrate:	10 g.	Sodium:	164 mg.

Peas Prosciutto

10 ounces mushrooms, sliced
¼ pound prosciutto, diced
1 medium onion, chopped
4 cloves garlic, minced
1 tablespoon olive oil
2 packages (10 ounces) frozen petite peas, thawed and drained
¼ teaspoon oregano
¼ teaspoon basil
¼ teaspoon pepper

Makes 8 servings

Place mushrooms in a 1-quart casserole; cover. Microwave at HIGH (100%) until tender, 3 to 4 minutes. Drain and set aside.

Place prosciutto, onions, garlic and olive oil in 2-quart casserole; cover. Microwave at HIGH (100%) until sautéed, 2 to 3 minutes. Toss in peas, spices and mushrooms. Microwave at HIGH (100%) until heated throughout, 3 to 4 minutes.

Per Serving:			
Calories:	113	Fat:	4 g.
Protein:	8 g.	Cholesterol:	12 mg.
Carbohydrate:	12 g.	Sodium:	360 mg.

Sweet Potato Casserole ▲

  4 medium sweet potatoes or yams
      (about 2 pounds)
  2 tablespoons water
¼ cup packed brown sugar
¼ cup margarine or butter
½ teaspoon salt
½ teaspoon ground cinnamon
¼ teaspoon nutmeg
  1 can (8 ounces) crushed pineapple
1½ cups miniature marshmallows
¼ cup chopped pecans

Makes 6 servings

Peel and slice potatoes. Place in 3-quart casserole with water. Microwave at HIGH (100%) until fork-tender, 8 to 11 minutes, stirring halfway through cooking. Cover and let stand 5 minutes. Add brown sugar, margarine and the spices. Mash until no lumps remain. Mix in pineapple.

Top sweet potato mixture with marshmallows. Microwave at HIGH (100%) until marshmallows are melted and potatoes are heated through, 3 to 6 minutes. Sprinkle with pecans.

Per Serving:			
Calories:	307	Fat:	11 g.
Protein:	3 g.	Cholesterol:	–
Carbohydrate:	52 g.	Sodium:	294 mg.

Acorn Squash with Cranberry Filling ▶

  2 large acorn squash (about 2 pounds each)
  1 can (16 ounces) whole cranberry sauce
  2 tablespoons orange juice
  2 tablespoons brown sugar
½ teaspoon ground cinnamon

Makes 4 servings

Prick squash several times with fork to allow steam to escape. Place in oven. Microwave at HIGH (100%) until soft when pricked with fork, 11 to 13 minutes, turning squash over and rotating after half the cooking time. Let stand 5 minutes. Cut in half and remove seeds. Place cut side up in 10-inch square casserole. Set aside.

Combine cranberry sauce, juice, brown sugar and cinnamon in small bowl. Microwave at HIGH (100%) until hot and bubbly, 2 to 3 minutes, stirring after half the cooking time. Spoon into squash halves. Microwave at HIGH (100%) until heated through, 1 to 2 minutes.

Per Serving:			
Calories:	339	Fat:	1 g.
Protein:	3 g.	Cholesterol:	–
Carbohydrate:	88 g.	Sodium:	45 mg.

Squash Parmesan

  3 small yellow summer squash (about 1 pound),
      thinly sliced
¼ cup chopped onion
  2 tablespoons water
  2 tablespoons grated fresh Parmesan cheese

Makes 4 servings

Place squash, onion and water in 1-quart casserole; cover. Microwave at HIGH (100%) until vegetables are tender, 3 to 6 minutes.

Sprinkle with Parmesan cheese. Microwave at HIGH (100%) until cheese melts, 1 to 2 minutes.

Per Serving:			
Calories:	32	Fat:	1 g.
Protein:	2 g.	Cholesterol:	2 mg.
Carbohydrate:	4 g.	Sodium:	60 mg.

PASTA, GRAINS & CEREALS

Help your family eat right by preparing delicious pasta and rice dishes and steaming hot cereals in your Sharp microwave oven. Cleanups for hot cereals, rice and pasta dishes are easy . . . no scrubbing!

**Hot Pasta Salad,
page 103**

Oatmeal with Prunes and Raisins

2½ cups hot water
1⅓ cups old-fashioned rolled oats
¼ cup instant nonfat dry milk powder
¼ cup chopped pitted prunes
2 tablespoons raisins
2 teaspoons margarine or butter
¼ teaspoon salt
¼ teaspoon ground cinnamon

Makes 4 servings

In 2-quart casserole, combine all ingredients. Mix well. Microwave at HIGH (100%) for 6 to 8 minutes or until desired consistency, stirring after half the time.

Per Serving:
Calories: 183 | Fat: 4 g.
Protein: 7 g. | Cholesterol: 1 mg.
Carbohydrate: 32 g. | Sodium: 194 mg.

Cereal Cooking Chart

Power Level: HIGH (100%)

Select a large bowl or casserole when microwaving cereals which boil over easily. Stir cereal once during cooking and again before serving.

	Amount	Salt (tsp.)	Water (cups)	Time (min.)
Quick Oatmeal				
1 serving	⅓ cup	¼	¾	1-2
4 servings	1⅓ cups	¾	3	4-5
Old-Fashioned Oatmeal				
1 serving	⅓ cup	¼	¾	3-5
4 servings	1⅓ cups	1	2½	6-8
Regular Cream of Wheat				
1 serving	2½ tbsp.	⅛	1	1-3
4 servings	⅔ cup	½	3½	7-10
Oat Bran				
1 serving	⅓ cup	⅛	1	1-2
4 servings	1⅓ cups	½	3-4	6-9

Spiced Creamy Cereal

2 cups skim milk
⅓ cup regular cream of wheat cereal
2 tablespoons chopped dried apricots
⅛ teaspoon salt
Dash ground nutmeg
Dash ground allspice

Makes 2 servings

In 2-quart casserole, combine all ingredients. Microwave at HIGH (100%) for 4 to 6 minutes or until cereal thickens, stirring after every 2 minutes.

Per Serving:
Calories: 141 | Fat: 1 g.
Protein: 10 g. | Cholesterol: 4 mg.
Carbohydrate: 24 g. | Sodium: 261 mg.

Sunny Couscous Cereal

¾ cup water
¼ cup fresh orange juice
½ cup uncooked couscous
1 teaspoon grated orange peel
2 tablespoons finely chopped blanched almonds
1 tablespoon honey
1 tablespoon frozen apple juice concentrate
Dash of ground cinnamon

Makes 4 servings

Combine all ingredients in 1-quart casserole. Cover. Microwave at HIGH (100%) until liquid is absorbed and couscous is tender, 5 to 6 minutes. Let stand, covered, 1 minute.

Per Serving:
Calories: 122 | Fat: 2 g.
Protein: 3 g. | Cholesterol: —
Carbohydrate: 23 g. | Sodium: 1 mg.

Spanish Rice with Shrimp ▶

1 can (16 ounces) stewed tomatoes
1½ cups water
⅔ cup uncooked long grain rice
⅓ cup finely chopped onion
¼ cup chopped celery
3 tablespoons tomato paste
¼ teaspoon salt
1 teaspoon sugar
1 teaspoon instant chicken bouillon
½ teaspoon dried oregano leaves
¼ to ½ teaspoon garlic powder
1 can (4½ ounces) small shrimp, rinsed and drained

Makes 8 servings

Combine all ingredients except shrimp in 3-quart casserole. Mix well. Cover. Microwave at HIGH (100%) 10 minutes. Reduce power to MEDIUM (50%). Microwave until liquid is absorbed and rice is tender, 28 to 35 minutes. Stir in shrimp. Let stand, covered, 5 minutes. Fluff with fork before serving.

Per Serving:			
Calories:	101	Fat:	1 g.
Protein:	6 g.	Cholesterol:	28 mg.
Carbohydrate:	19 g.	Sodium:	337 mg.

Instant Rice

1¼ cups uncooked instant rice
1¼ cups hot water
1 teaspoon salt
1 teaspoon margarine or butter (optional)

Makes 4 servings

Combine all ingredients in 3-quart casserole. Cover. Microwave at HIGH (100%) until water boils, 4 to 6 minutes. Let stand, covered, 5 minutes. Fluff with fork before serving.

Per Serving:			
Calories:	111	Fat:	—
Protein:	2 g.	Cholesterol:	—
Carbohydrate:	25 g.	Sodium:	533 mg.

Brown Rice

1 cup parboiled long grain brown rice
2¾ cups hot water
1 tablespoon margarine or butter (optional)
½ teaspoon salt

Makes 4 servings

Combine all ingredients in 3-quart casserole. Cover. Microwave at HIGH (100%) 5 minutes. Reduce power to MEDIUM (50%). Microwave until liquid is absorbed and rice is tender, 35 to 45 minutes. Let stand 5 minutes. Fluff with fork before serving.

Per Serving:			
Calories:	167	Fat:	1 g.
Protein:	3 g.	Cholesterol:	—
Carbohydrate:	36 g.	Sodium:	271 mg.

Long Grain Rice

1 cup uncooked long grain rice
2 cups hot water
1 tablespoon margarine or butter (optional)
1 teaspoon salt

Makes 4 servings

Combine all ingredients in 3-quart casserole. Cover. Microwave at HIGH (100%) 5 minutes. Reduce power to MEDIUM (50%). Microwave until liquid is absorbed and rice is tender, 9 to 11 minutes. Fluff with fork before serving.

Per Serving:			
Calories:	168	Fat:	—
Protein:	3 g.	Cholesterol:	—
Carbohydrate:	37 g.	Sodium:	535 mg.

Rice Oregano ▲

1 can (13¾ ounces) chicken broth
1 cup uncooked long grain rice
¼ cup finely chopped onion
2 tablespoons margarine or butter
¾ teaspoon dried oregano leaves
⅛ teaspoon pepper

Makes 6 servings

Combine all ingredients in 3-quart casserole. Mix well. Cover. Microwave at HIGH (100%) 5 minutes. Reduce power to MEDIUM (50%). Microwave until liquid is absorbed and rice is tender, 13 to 16 minutes. Let stand, covered, 5 minutes. Fluff with fork before serving.

Per Serving:			
Calories:	160	Fat:	5 g.
Protein:	3 g.	Cholesterol:	2 mg.
Carbohydrate:	25 g.	Sodium:	425 mg.

Rice Pilaf ▲

½ cup chopped onion
½ cup sliced celery
½ cup chopped green pepper
2 tablespoons margarine or butter
1 can (13¾ ounces) chicken broth
1 can (4 ounces) sliced mushrooms, drained
1 cup uncooked long grain rice

Makes 6 servings

Combine onion, celery, green pepper and margarine in 1-quart casserole. Microwave at HIGH (100%) until vegetables are tender-crisp, 3 to 5 minutes. Stir in remaining ingredients; cover.

Microwave at HIGH (100%) 5 minutes. Reduce power to MEDIUM (50%). Microwave until liquid is absorbed, 13 to 16 minutes. Let stand, covered, 5 minutes. Fluff with fork before serving.

Per Serving:			
Calories:	168	Fat:	5 g.
Protein:	3 g.	Cholesterol:	2 mg.
Carbohydrate:	27 g.	Sodium:	477 mg.

Fried Rice

4 tablespoons chopped green onion
1 tablespoon margarine or butter
1 can (13¾ ounces) chicken broth
2 cups uncooked instant rice
2 eggs, beaten
2 tablespoons soy sauce

Makes 6 servings

Combine onion and margarine in 3-quart casserole. Microwave at HIGH (100%) until onion is tender, 1 to 2 minutes.

Add broth and rice to casserole; cover. Microwave at HIGH (100%) until mixture boils, 4 to 6 minutes. Let stand, covered, until liquid is absorbed, 5 to 6 minutes.

Stir in eggs and soy sauce. Microwave, uncovered, at HIGH (100%) until eggs are set, 2 to 3 minutes, stirring several times during cooking. Fluff with fork before serving.

Per Serving:			
Calories:	176	Fat:	5 g.
Protein:	5 g.	Cholesterol:	72 mg.
Carbohydrate:	28 g.	Sodium:	767 mg.

Mushroom Tetrazzini ▶

1 package (1 pound) spaghetti
¼ cup margarine or butter
1 cup sliced fresh mushrooms
½ cup chopped onion
¼ cup all-purpose flour
2 tablespoons sherry
½ teaspoon salt
⅛ teaspoon pepper
1½ cups milk
4 ounces Provolone cheese,
    cut into ¼-inch cubes
4 ounces mozzarella cheese,
    cut into ¼-inch cubes

Makes 6 servings

Prepare spaghetti as directed on package. Rinse and drain. Cover. Set aside. Combine margarine, mushrooms and onion in 3-quart casserole. Microwave at HIGH (100%) until mushrooms are tender, 2 to 3 minutes, stirring once. Stir in flour, sherry, salt and pepper. Blend in milk. Microwave at HIGH (100%) until mixture thickens and bubbles, 6 to 8 minutes, stirring every 2 minutes. Stir in Provolone and mozzarella cheeses. Microwave at HIGH (100%) until mixture can be stirred smooth, 1½ to 2 minutes, stirring after every minute. Pour cheese mixture over spaghetti. Toss to coat. Microwave at HIGH (100%) until heated through, 1 to 2 minutes.

Per Serving:			
Calories:	540	Fat:	20 g.
Protein:	21 g.	Cholesterol:	36 mg.
Carbohydrate:	67 g.	Sodium:	544 mg.

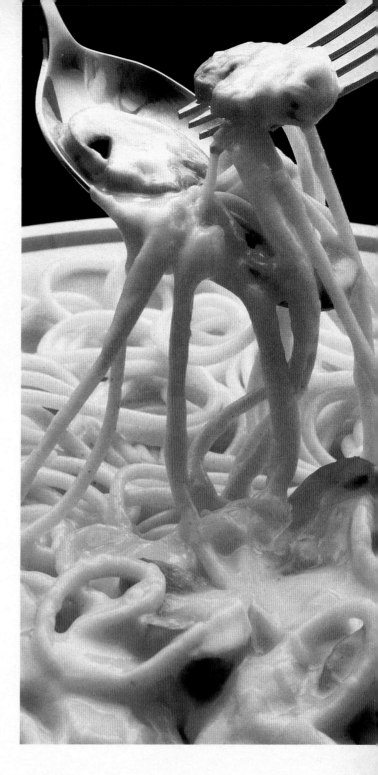

Hot Pasta Salad

1 medium green pepper, cut into ¼-inch strips
½ medium red onion, cut in half lengthwise and thinly sliced
2 tablespoons margarine or butter
2 teaspoons poppy seed
⅛ teaspoon salt
¾ cup cooked spaghetti
1 medium tomato, cut into thin wedges

Makes 4 servings

Combine all ingredients except spaghetti and tomato in 1-quart casserole. Cover. Microwave at HIGH (100%) until pepper and onion are tender, 3 to 5 minutes, stirring once. Add remaining ingredients. Toss lightly. Re-cover. Microwave at HIGH (100%) until hot, 2 to 3 minutes. Let stand, covered, 1 minute.

Per Serving:			
Calories:	110	Fat:	7 g.
Protein:	2 g.	Cholesterol:	—
Carbohydrate:	11 g.	Sodium:	137 mg.

Cheese-Stuffed Manicotti ▲

8 uncooked manicotti shells

Sauce:
- 1 can (8 ounces) whole tomatoes, undrained and cut up
- 1 can (8 ounces) tomato sauce
- 1 tablespoon Burgundy wine
- 2 teaspoons olive oil
- ½ teaspoon dried basil leaves
- ½ teaspoon onion powder
- ½ teaspoon oregano
- ¼ teaspoon garlic powder

Filling:
- 1 carton (15 ounces) lite ricotta cheese (1 gram fat per ounce)
- 2 eggs
- ¼ cup grated Parmesan cheese
- 2 tablespoons snipped parsley
- ½ teaspoon garlic powder
- ½ cup shredded mozzarella cheese

Makes 4 servings

Prepare manicotti shells as directed on package. Rinse. Let stand in warm water while preparing sauce and filling.

Combine sauce ingredients in 2-quart casserole. Microwave at HIGH (100%), uncovered, until flavors are blended and sauce is slightly thickened, 6 to 8 minutes, stirring twice. Set aside.

Combine filling ingredients in small mixing bowl. Stuff each cooked manicotti shell with scant ⅓ cup cheese filling.

Reserve ⅓ cup tomato sauce. Set aside. Pour remaining sauce into 8-inch round casserole. Arrange stuffed shells in sauce. Spoon reserved sauce over manicotti. Cover. Microwave at MEDIUM-HIGH (70%) until hot, 12 to 14 minutes. Sprinkle with mozzarella. Let stand, covered, until cheese melts, 5 minutes.

Per Serving:					
Calories:	341	Carbohydrate:	31 g.	Cholesterol:	137 mg.
Protein:	24 g.	Fat:	14 g.	Sodium:	691 mg.

Fresh Vegetable Alfredo

- ½ pound fresh asparagus, cut into ¾-inch lengths
- ¼ cup margarine or butter
- 1 can (16 ounces) pitted black olives, drained
- ½ cup whipping cream
- 2 eggs, beaten
- ½ cup grated Parmesan cheese
- ⅛ teaspoon garlic powder
- ⅛ teaspoon pepper
- 8 ounces uncooked fettucini
- 1 cup quartered cherry tomatoes

Makes 4 servings

Place asparagus and margarine in 2-quart casserole. Cover. Microwave at HIGH (100%) until margarine is melted and asparagus is tender-crisp, 3 to 4 minutes, stirring once. Add olives. Set aside. Blend whipping cream, eggs, Parmesan cheese, garlic powder and pepper in small mixing bowl. Add to asparagus mixture. Mix well. Set aside.

Prepare fettucini as directed on package. Rinse and drain. Add to asparagus mixture. Toss to coat. Microwave at MEDIUM (50%) until hot, 4 to 6 minutes, stirring every 2 minutes. Add cherry tomatoes. Toss to combine. Before serving, sprinkle with additional grated Parmesan cheese, if desired.

Per Serving:	
Calories:	583
Protein:	19 g.
Carbohydrate:	49 g.
Fat:	36 g.
Cholesterol:	188 mg.
Sodium:	749 mg.

White Lasagna Primavera ▲

12 uncooked lasagna noodles
 1 cup fresh broccoli flowerets
 1 cup sliced fresh mushrooms
 1 cup sliced yellow summer squash
 1 cup sliced zucchini
 1 cup chopped onion
¼ cup shredded carrots
 3 large garlic cloves, minced
 2 cartons (15 ounces each) ricotta cheese
½ teaspoon salt
½ teaspoon pepper
 1 teaspoon garlic powder
 2 teaspoons oregano
 2 teaspoons dried basil
 1 teaspoon onion powder
 2 eggs
 3 tablespoons chopped fresh parsley
 2 cups shredded white Cheddar cheese
¼ cup Parmesan cheese

Makes 8 servings

Prepare lasagna noodles as directed on package. Rinse. Let stand in warm water.

Combine fresh vegetables, onion and garlic in 3-quart casserole; cover. Microwave at High (100%) until vegetables are tender, 10 to 12 minutes, stirring once. Drain well. Drain squash and zucchini on paper towels.

In medium bowl, combine ricotta cheese with spices, eggs, parsley, 1 cup of Cheddar cheese and Parmesan cheese. Set aside.

Place lasagna noodles on paper towel to drain and cut in half crosswise. Spray two 8-inch round or square baking dishes with nonstick spray.

Layer 4 noodles, ¼ of vegetables and ¼ of ricotta mixture in first dish. Top with 4 noodles, ¼ of vegetables and ¼ of ricotta mixture. Top with 4 noodles and ½ cup of Cheddar cheese. Repeat with second dish.

Cover with plastic wrap. Microwave at MEDIUM-HIGH (70%) until hot, 10 to 12 minutes. Let stand, covered, 10 minutes. Repeat with second dish.

Per Serving:			
Calories:	500	Fat:	26 g.
Protein:	28 g.	Cholesterol:	139 mg.
Carbohydrate:	38 g.	Sodium:	475 mg.

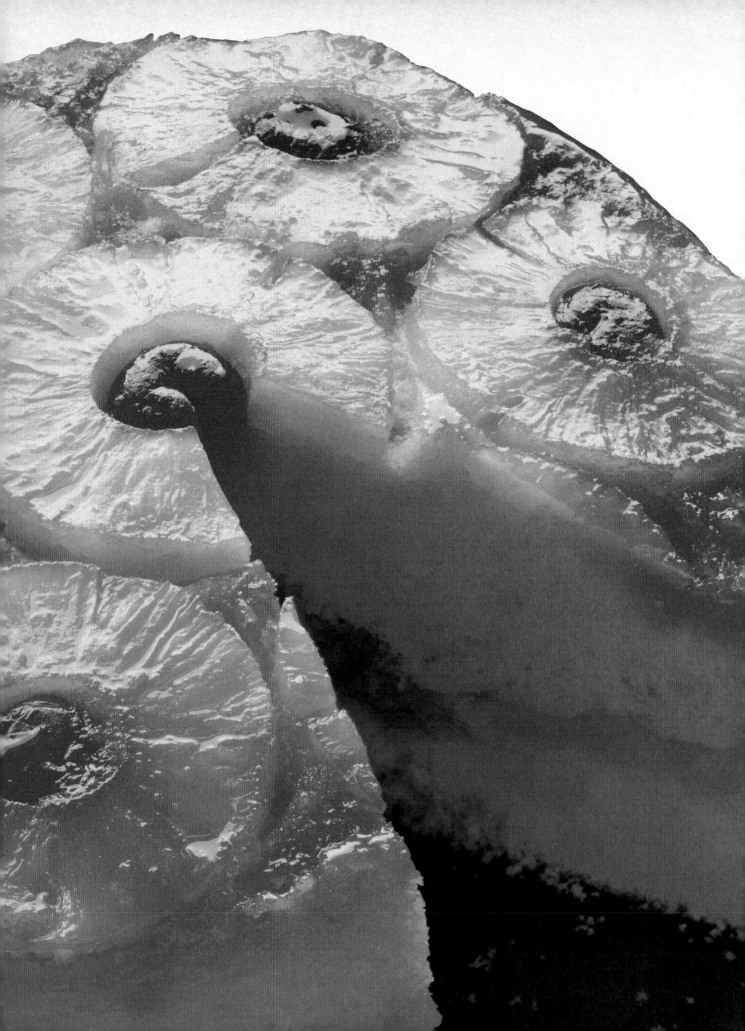

BAKING & DESSERTS

There's a happy ending to a perfect meal when you use your microwave oven to prepare homemade favorites, such as puddings, cheesecakes and cobblers that bring back memories of your grandmother's kitchen. Use the microwave oven for melting chocolate or butter or toasting nuts or coconut.

Two-Layer Pineapple Upside-Down Cake

1 can (15½ ounces) crushed pineapple (juice pack), drained (reserve juice)
1 tablespoon cornstarch
2 tablespoons packed brown sugar
1 tablespoon honey
½ teaspoon lemon juice
2 tablespoons margarine or butter
¼ cup packed brown sugar
1 can (8 ounces) pineapple slices (juice pack), drained (reserve juice)
7 maraschino cherries, drained
1 package (18½ ounces) yellow cake mix

Makes 12 servings

Blend juice from crushed pineapple and cornstarch in small bowl. Stir in crushed pineapple, 2 tablespoons brown sugar, the honey and lemon juice. Microwave at HIGH (100%) until thickened, 4 to 5 minutes, stirring after half the time. Set aside. Place margarine in round baking dish, 9 × 1½ inches. Microwave at HIGH (100%) until melted, 30 to 45 seconds. Stir in ¼ cup brown sugar; spread evenly in dish. Arrange pineapple slices and cherries over brown sugar. Set aside.

Line round baking dish, 9 × 1½ inches, with wax paper. Add enough additional water to juice reserved from pineapple slices to equal amount of water needed for preparing cake mix. Prepare cake mix according to package directions using pineapple juice-water mixture. Pour half of the batter into wax paper-lined baking dish and half over pineapple slices.

Microwave first layer (wax paper-lined baking dish) at MEDIUM-HIGH (70%) 5 minutes. Increase power to HIGH (100%). Microwave until wooden pick inserted in center comes out clean, 1 to 4 minutes. Invert onto serving plate; spread with crushed pineapple mixture. Microwave pineapple layer at MEDIUM-HIGH (70%) 4 minutes. Increase power to HIGH (100%). Microwave until wooden pick inserted in center comes out clean, 3 to 6 minutes. Cool 2 minutes. Invert second layer on top of first.

Per Serving:			
Calories:	381	Fat:	18 g.
Protein:	4 g.	Cholesterol:	69 mg.
Carbohydrate:	53 g.	Sodium:	220 mg.

Carrot Bread

½ cup whole wheat flour
½ cup all-purpose flour
½ cup granulated sugar
¼ cup packed brown sugar
½ teaspoon baking soda
½ teaspoon baking powder
½ teaspoon salt
1 teaspoon cinnamon
½ cup vegetable oil
2 eggs
1 teaspoon vanilla
2 cups grated carrots
⅓ cup raisins (optional)

Makes 12 servings

Lightly grease loaf dish, 9 X 5 inches. Combine flours, sugars, baking soda, baking powder, salt and cinnamon in medium mixing bowl. Add remaining ingredients except carrots and raisins. Beat at low speed until just blended. Stir in carrots and raisins. Pour into loaf dish. Cover ends of loaf dish with 2-inch strips of foil and mold to fit around handles.

Place dish on saucer or roasting rack in oven. Microwave at MEDIUM (50%) 9 to 10 minutes. Remove foil and microwave at HIGH (100%) until bread just begins to pull away from the edges of the dish, no uncooked batter can be seen through bottom of dish and wooden pick inserted in center comes out clean, 2 to 4 minutes. Cool directly on countertop 10 minutes. Remove from dish. Store in refrigerator.

Per Serving:			
Calories:	187	Fat:	10 g.
Protein:	2 g.	Cholesterol:	46 mg.
Carbohydrate:	22 g.	Sodium:	227 mg.

Chocolate Chip Zucchini Cake ▶

½ cup margarine or butter
1 cup sugar
1 cup all-purpose flour
2 tablespoons cocoa
½ teaspoon baking soda
¼ teaspoon baking powder
¼ teaspoon ground cinnamon
1 cup shredded zucchini
¼ cup buttermilk
1 egg
1 teaspoon vanilla
½ cup semisweet chocolate chips

Frosting:
¼ cup margarine or butter
3 ounces cream cheese
1¼ cups powdered sugar
½ teaspoon vanilla

Makes 8 servings

Place margarine in medium mixing bowl. Microwave at HIGH (100%) until softened, 15 seconds. Add sugar and beat at medium speed of electric mixer until light and fluffy. Add remaining cake ingredients except chocolate chips. Beat at low speed until

moistened. Beat at medium speed 1 minute, scraping bowl occasionally. Stir in chocolate chips. Spread batter into 8-inch round baking dish.

Place dish on saucer in microwave oven. Microwave at MEDIUM (50%) 7 to 9 minutes. Increase power to HIGH (100%). Microwave until top appears dry and center springs back when lightly touched, 2 to 3 minutes. Let stand covered on counter until cooled.

Place margarine and cream cheese in medium bowl. Microwave at HIGH (100%) until softened, 30 seconds. Add powdered sugar and vanilla. Beat at high speed of electric mixer until smooth. Refrigerate. Spread frosting over top of cooled cake.

Per Serving:			
Calories:	486	Fat:	25 g.
Protein:	4 g.	Cholesterol:	38 mg.
Carbohydrate:	65 g.	Sodium:	343 mg.

Hearty Bran Muffins

2½ cups raisin bran cereal
1½ cups buttermilk
1¼ cups flour
½ cup packed brown sugar
1 tablespoon baking powder
½ teaspoon salt
¼ teaspoon ground cinnamon
¼ cup vegetable oil
1 egg

Makes 2 dozen

Mix cereal and buttermilk in medium bowl. Let stand until all liquid is absorbed. Combine flour, sugar, baking powder, salt and cinnamon. Stir oil and egg into cereal mixture; add flour mixture. Mix only until evenly moistened.

Spoon batter into paper-lined microwave muffin pan, filling each ½ full. Microwave 6 muffins at MEDIUM (50%) until wooden pick inserted at center comes out clean, 4½ to 5½ minutes. Repeat with remaining batter.

Per Serving:			
Calories:	86	Fat:	3 g.
Protein:	2 g.	Cholesterol:	9 mg.
Carbohydrate:	14 g.	Sodium:	164 mg.

Apple Crisp ▶

4 cups sliced peeled apples
2 tablespoons lemon juice
½ cup packed brown sugar
½ cup uncooked quick-cooking or old-fashioned oats
¼ cup all-purpose flour
¼ cup margarine or butter
1 teaspoon ground cinnamon
½ teaspoon salt
⅛ teaspoon ground nutmeg

Makes 6 servings

Place apples in 1-quart casserole. Sprinkle with lemon juice. Microwave at HIGH (100%) until apples are tender-crisp, 2½ to 4 minutes. Set apples aside.

Combine remaining ingredients in small bowl. Microwave at HIGH (100%) until hot and bubbly, 1½ to 3½ minutes, stirring after half the cooking time. Spread over apples. Microwave at HIGH (100%) until apples are tender and topping is bubbly, 3 to 5 minutes.

Per Serving:			
Calories:	227	Fat:	8 g.
Protein:	1 g.	Cholesterol:	—
Carbohydrate:	39 g.	Sodium:	273 mg.

Pots de Crème ▲

2 squares (1 ounce each) unsweetened chocolate, broken
1 cup light cream
⅔ cup sugar
2 egg yolks, slightly beaten
2 tablespoons butter, softened
1 teaspoon vanilla
Whipped cream for garnish

Makes 4 servings

Combine chocolate and cream in a 4-cup measure or bowl. Microwave at MEDIUM (50%) until chocolate flecks disappear and mixture boils, 4 to 6 minutes, whisking very well halfway through cooking. Add sugar and stir well. Microwave at MEDIUM (50%), until mixture begins to boil, 1½ to 2 minutes. Add chocolate to eggs, whisking quickly. Stir in butter and vanilla. Pour into individual cups, cover and chill several hours. Garnish with whipped cream.

Per Serving:			
Calories:	404	Fat:	28 g.
Protein:	5 g.	Cholesterol:	161 mg.
Carbohydrate:	40 g.	Sodium:	88 mg.

Cherry Cobbler

6 tablespoons margarine or butter
1 cup all-purpose flour
⅔ cup coarsely chopped nuts
⅓ cup packed dark brown sugar
¾ teaspoon ground cinnamon
¼ teaspoon ground allspice
1 can (21 ounces) cherry pie filling
2 teaspoons cornstarch
½ teaspoon lemon juice

Makes 6 servings

Place margarine in small bowl. Microwave at HIGH (100%) until melted, 45 seconds to 1 minute 15 seconds. Stir in flour, nuts, brown sugar, cinnamon and allspice. Set topping aside.

Mix cherry pie filling, cornstarch and lemon juice until smooth in 1-quart casserole. Microwave at HIGH (100%) 1 minute. Sprinkle with topping. Reduce power to MEDIUM-HIGH (70%). Microwave until filling is translucent and bubbly, 5 to 8 minutes. Serve warm or cold with ice cream or whipped topping, if desired.

Per Serving:			
Calories:	608	Fat:	20 g.
Protein:	4 g.	Cholesterol:	—
Carbohydrate:	105 g.	Sodium:	165 mg.

Cinnamon Baked Apples

4 large baking apples (2½- to 3-inch diameter)
4 tablespoons red cinnamon candies

Makes 4 servings

Core apples without cutting through bottom skin and peel about 1-inch strip of skin from stem end of each apple. If necessary, cut thin slice from bottom of each apple so it will stand upright.

Arrange apples in shallow baking dish. Place 1 tablespoon of the cinnamon candies in center of each apple. Microwave at HIGH (100%) until apples are tender, 4 to 6 minutes.

Per Serving:
Calories:	150
Protein:	—
Carbohydrate:	38 g.
Fat:	1 g.
Cholesterol:	—
Sodium:	30 mg.

Deep Dish Apple Pie ▲

1 tablespoon sugar
½ teaspoon ground cinnamon
5 cups sliced peeled apples
½ cup sugar
2 tablespoons all-purpose flour
½ teaspoon ground cinnamon or cloves
¾ cup buttermilk biscuit baking mix
⅓ cup milk
2 tablespoons sugar

Makes 6 servings

Mix 1 tablespoon sugar and ½ teaspoon cinnamon; set aside. Combine apples, ½ cup sugar, the flour and ½ teaspoon cinnamon or cloves in 1-quart casserole. Cover. Microwave at HIGH (100%) until apples are tender and sauce is bubbly, 3 to 5 minutes.

Mix buttermilk biscuit baking mix, milk and 2 tablespoons sugar just until moistened. Drop by spoonfuls onto hot apple mixture. Sprinkle with cinnamon-sugar mixture. Microwave at HIGH (100%) until topping is set, 4 to 6 minutes. Serve with whipped cream, if desired.

Per Serving:
Calories:	217	Fat:	3 g.
Protein:	2 g.	Cholesterol:	1 mg.
Carbohydrate:	48 g.	Sodium:	182 mg.

Graham Cracker Crust ▲

3 tablespoons margarine or butter
1 cup fine graham cracker crumbs
¼ cup granulated or packed brown sugar

Makes 9-inch pie crust,
6 servings

Place margarine in 9-inch pie plate. Microwave at HIGH (100%) until melted, 30 seconds to 1 minute. Add graham cracker crumbs and sugar; mix thoroughly. Press mixture firmly against bottom and side of pie plate.

Microwave at MEDIUM-HIGH (70%) until hot, 2 to 4 minutes. Cool completely before filling.

Chocolate Cookie Crust Variation: Follow recipe for Graham Cracker Crust, except increase margarine to ¼ cup and substitute 1¼ cups fine chocolate wafer cookie crumbs for graham cracker curmbs and brown sugar.

Per Serving:			
Calories:	140	Fat:	7 g.
Protein:	1 g.	Cholesterol:	—
Carbohydrate:	19 g.	Sodium:	165 mg.

Baked Pie Shell ▲

1 cup flour
½ teaspoon salt
3 tablespoons shortening
3 tablespoons butter
3 tablespoons ice water

Makes 1 9-inch pie shell
6 servings

Mix flour and salt. Cut in shortening and butter with knife until particles are size of small peas. Add water and toss with fork. Shape into ball. Between 2 pieces of wax paper, roll to a 13-inch circle. Place in 9-inch pie plate. Let rest 10 minutes.

Trim overhanging edge of pastry to generous ½ inch. Fold under, even with plate, to form standing rim. Flute, keeping rim high to contain bubbling. Prick crust with fork on bottom and side ½ inch apart. Microwave at HIGH (100%) until crust appears dry and opaque through bottom of plate, 4 to 5½ minutes.

Per Serving:			
Calories:	183	Fat:	12 g.
Protein:	2 g.	Cholesterol:	16 mg.
Carbohydrate:	16 g.	Sodium:	241 mg.

Applesauce

4 cups sliced peeled tart apples
¼ cup water
¼ to ½ cup sugar
¼ teaspoon ground cinnamon

Makes 6 servings

Place all ingredients in 2-quart casserole; cover.

Microwave at HIGH (100%) until apples are tender, 7 to 10 minutes. Mash apples to desired consistency. Serve warm or chilled.

Per Serving:			
Calories:	74	Fat:	–
Protein:	–	Cholesterol:	–
Carbohydrate:	19 g.	Sodium:	–

Cheesecake ▾

Graham Cracker Crust (page 113)
2 packages (8 ounces each) cream cheese, softened
½ cup sugar
2 eggs, separated
1 tablespoon lemon juice
1 teaspoon grated lemon peel
½ cup dairy sour cream
1 tablespoon sugar
½ teaspoon vanilla

Makes 8 servings

Prepare crust. Set aside. Beat cream cheese and ½ cup sugar in large mixing bowl until light and fluffy. Beat in egg yolks, lemon juice and peel until smooth.

Beat egg whites in small mixing bowl until stiff peaks form. Fold beaten egg whites into cream cheese mixture. Spread evenly in prepared crust.

Microwave at MEDIUM (50%) until center is set, 8 to 10 minutes. Refrigerate several hours before serving. Mix sour cream, 1 tablespoon sugar and the vanilla. Carefully spread over cheesecake before serving.

Per Serving:			
Calories:	408	Fat:	30 g.
Protein:	7 g.	Cholesterol:	138 mg.
Carbohydrate:	31 g.	Sodium:	315 mg.

Crème de Menthe Pie ▲

3 cups miniature marshmallows
⅓ cup half-and-half
¼ cup green crème de menthe
3 tablespoons white crème de cacao
Chocolate Cookie Crust (page 113)
1 cup chilled whipping cream

Makes 8 servings

Combine marshmallows and half-and-half in medium bowl. Microwave at MEDIUM-HIGH (70%) until marshmallows are melted, 2 to 4 minutes, stirring once or twice during cooking. Blend in crème de menthe and crème de cacao. Refrigerate until cool and thickened but not set. Prepare crust while filling cools.

When marshmallow mixture is thickened but not set, beat whipping cream in chilled bowl until stiff. Fold marshmallow mixture into whipped cream. Pour into crust. Refrigerate until set, 2 to 4 hours. Garnish with chocolate curls, if desired.

Per Serving:			
Calories:	274	Fat:	14 g.
Protein:	2 g.	Cholesterol:	29 mg.
Carbohydrate:	35 g.	Sodium:	102 mg.

Quick Cherry Pie ▲

Baked Pie Shell (page 113)
1 cup sugar
¼ cup cornstarch
⅛ teaspoon salt
2 cans (16 ounces each) pitted tart red cherries
(water pack), drained
½ teaspoon almond extract
⅓ cup sliced almonds

Makes 6 servings

Bake pie shell. Set aside. Blend sugar, cornstarch and salt in medium bowl. Stir in cherries.

Microwave at HIGH (100%) until mixture is translucent, 8 to 11 minutes, stirring once or twice during cooking. Stir in almond extract. Pour into pie shell. Sprinkle with almonds. Chill.

Per Serving:			
Calories:	448	Fat:	19 g.
Protein:	5 g.	Cholesterol:	—
Carbohydrate:	69 g.	Sodium:	279 mg.

Pumpkin Cheese Pie ▲

Graham Cracker Crust (page 113)
1 package (8 ounces) cream cheese
1 cup canned pumpkin
¾ cup packed brown sugar
3 eggs
1½ tablespoons all-purpose flour
1 teaspoon ground cinnamon
½ teaspoon ground nutmeg
½ teaspoon vanilla

Makes 6 servings

Prepare crust. Set aside. Place cream cheese in medium bowl. Microwave at MEDIUM (50%) until softened, 1 to 2 minutes. Add remaining ingredients. Beat at medium speed of electric mixer until smooth and well blended.

Microwave at MEDIUM-HIGH (70%) until hot and thickened, 6 to 8 minutes, stirring every 2 minutes. Pour into crust. Reduce power to MEDIUM (50%). Microwave until filling is firm to the touch, 8 to 10 minutes. Center may appear soft-set. Garnish with pecan halves, if desired. Refrigerate until set.

Per Serving:			
Calories:	435	Fat:	23 g.
Protein:	8 g.	Cholesterol:	179 mg.
Carbohydrate:	52 g.	Sodium:	319 mg.

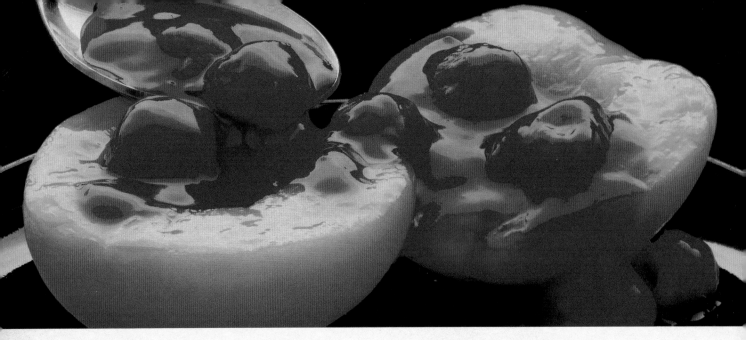

Peaches
with Raspberry Sauce ▲

1 package (10 ounces) frozen sweetened
   raspberries
4 peaches, peeled and cut into halves
2 teaspoons cornstarch
½ teaspoon grated lemon peel

Makes 4 servings

Remove raspberries from package and place in 1-quart container. Microwave at MEDIUM (50%) until raspberries are defrosted, 2 to 4 minutes, turning over every minute and gently breaking apart as soon as possible. Let stand 5 minutes.

Place peach halves in rectangular baking dish, 12 × 8 inches, or 10-inch square casserole. Cover with plastic wrap. Microwave at HIGH (100%) until peaches are heated through, 2 to 6 minutes. Set aside.

Drain raspberry juice in small bowl. Blend in cornstarch and lemon peel. Microwave at MEDIUM-HIGH (70%) until thick and bubbly, 2 to 4 minutes, stirring once or twice during cooking. Place 2 peach halves in each of 4 small bowls. Stir raspberries gently into sauce. Top each bowl of peaches with one-fourth of raspberry mixture. Top with whipped cream, if desired.

Variation: Substitute 8 canned peach halves and omit cooking peaches.

Per Serving:			
Calories:	97	Fat:	—
Protein:	1 g.	Cholesterol:	—
Carbohydrate:	25 g.	Sodium:	1 mg.

Bananas Foster

¼ cup butter
⅔ cup packed brown sugar
2 tablespoons milk
¼ teaspoon ground cinnamon
¼ teaspoon ground nutmeg
4 medium bananas, sliced
¼ cup light rum

Makes 6 servings

Combine all ingredients except bananas and rum in 1½-quart casserole. Microwave at HIGH (100%) until melted and bubbly, 1 to 1½ minutes, stirring once.

Add banana slices. Microwave at HIGH (100%) until bananas are warm, 45 seconds to 1 minute. Stir.

Pour rum into 1-cup measure or bowl. Microwave at HIGH (100%) 20 seconds. Light with a match and pour immediately over banana mixture. Stir until flaming stops. Serve over ice cream, if desired.

Variation: Serve over poundcake or waffles or in crepes. Top with whipped cream, nuts or toasted coconut.

Per Serving:			
Calories:	244	Fat:	8 g.
Protein:	1 g.	Cholesterol:	21 mg.
Carbohydrate:	42 g.	Sodium:	89 mg.

Chocolate Almond Fondue ▶

1 package (12 ounces) milk chocolate chips
2 tablespoons half-and-half
¼ cup almond liqueur
   Pound cake squares
   Ladyfingers, split
   Banana chunks, sprinkled with lemon juice
   Mandarin orange sections, drained
   Pineapple slices, drained and quartered

Makes 8 servings

Combine chocolate chips and half-and-half in small bowl or 1-quart casserole.

Microwave at MEDIUM-HIGH (70%) until chocolate is melted, 2 to 4 minutes, blending with wire whisk once or twice during cooking. Stir in liqueur. Serve from bowl, reheating as needed, or in fondue pot over low heat. Dip pound cake squares, ladyfingers, banana chunks, mandarin orange sections and pineapple slices into fondue with fondue forks or skewers.

Variation: Omit liqueur. Increase half-and-half to ⅓ cup. Add ½ teaspoon almond extract.

Per Serving:			
Calories:	244	Fat:	14 g.
Protein:	3 g.	Cholesterol:	10 mg.
Carbohydrate:	30 g.	Sodium:	40 mg.

Poached Pears

6 firm pears
2½ cups port wine
1½ cups sugar
1 lemon slice
3 cloves
1 cinnamon stick

Makes 6 servings

Peel, core, and halve pears. Set aside.

Combine remaining ingredients in 3-quart casserole. Microwave at HIGH (100%) until hot, 5 to 6 minutes, stirring halfway through cooking time.

Add pears; cover. Microwave at HIGH (100%) until fork-tender, 10 to 12 minutes.

Per Serving:			
Calories:	444	Fat:	1 g.
Protein:	1 g.	Cholesterol:	–
Carbohydrate:	87 g.	Sodium:	10 mg.

◄ Regal Chocolate Sauce

1 cup semisweet or milk chocolate chips
¼ cup light corn syrup
2 tablespoons milk
½ teaspoon salt
2 tablespoons butter
1 teaspoon vanilla

Makes 16 servings

Combine chocolate and corn syrup in 2-cup measure or small bowl. Microwave at MEDIUM (50%) until melted, 1 to 2 minutes. Stir.

Blend in milk and microwave at MEDIUM (50%) until smooth, 1 to 1½ minutes. Stir in salt, butter and vanilla until melted and smooth. Serve over cake or ice cream, if desired.

Variations: Stir in ½ teaspoon extract (peppermint, orange, almond). Or add 1 tablespoon of peanut butter and 2 tablespoons of milk, stirring until well blended.

Per Serving:			
Calories:	80	Fat:	4 g.
Protein:	1 g.	Cholesterol:	4 mg.
Carbohydrate:	11 g.	Sodium:	92 mg.

Hot Vanilla Sauce

½ cup packed brown sugar
1 tablespoon plus 1½ teaspoons all-purpose flour
    Dash of ground nutmeg
½ cup milk
¾ cup half-and-half
1½ teaspoons vanilla or rum extract

Makes 8 servings

Combine sugar, flour and nutmeg in medium bowl. Stir in ¼ cup of the milk until smooth. Stir in remaining milk and half-and-half.

Microwave at HIGH (100%) until thickened, 4 to 6 minutes, stirring 2 or 3 times. Stir in vanilla. Serve over cake or fruit, if desired.

Per Serving:			
Calories:	94	Fat:	3 g.
Protein:	1 g.	Cholesterol:	10 mg.
Carbohydrate:	16 g.	Sodium:	21 mg.

Lemon Sauce ▸

½ cup sugar
1 tablespoon cornstarch
Dash of salt
½ teaspoon grated lemon peel
1 cup water
1 tablespoon lemon juice
2 tablespoons margarine or butter
1 egg yolk, slightly beaten

Makes 8 servings

Combine sugar, cornstarch, salt and lemon peel in deep 1-quart bowl. Blend in water and lemon juice.

Microwave at HIGH (100%) until sauce is thickened and clear, 2 to 4 minutes, stirring after half the cooking time. Stir in margarine and egg yolk. Microwave at HIGH (100%) until bubbly, 30 seconds to 1 minute.

Per Serving:			
Calories:	86	Fat:	4 g.
Protein:	—	Cholesterol:	34 mg.
Carbohydrate:	14 g.	Sodium:	51 mg.

Cherry Sauce

1 can (17 ounces) pitted dark sweet cherries
1 tablespoon cornstarch
1½ teaspoons lemon juice
1 teaspoon grated lemon peel

Makes 8 servings

Drain cherry juice into 1-quart bowl; blend in cornstarch until smooth. Microwave at HIGH (100%) until clear and thickened, 2½ to 4 minutes, stirring once during cooking.

Stir in cherries, lemon juice and peel. Microwave at HIGH (100%) until sauce bubbles and cherries are hot, 1 to 2 minutes. (For thicker sauce add 1 teaspoon additional cornstarch.)

Per Serving:			
Calories:	36	Fat:	—
Protein:	1 g.	Cholesterol:	—
Carbohydrate:	9 g.	Sodium:	2 mg.

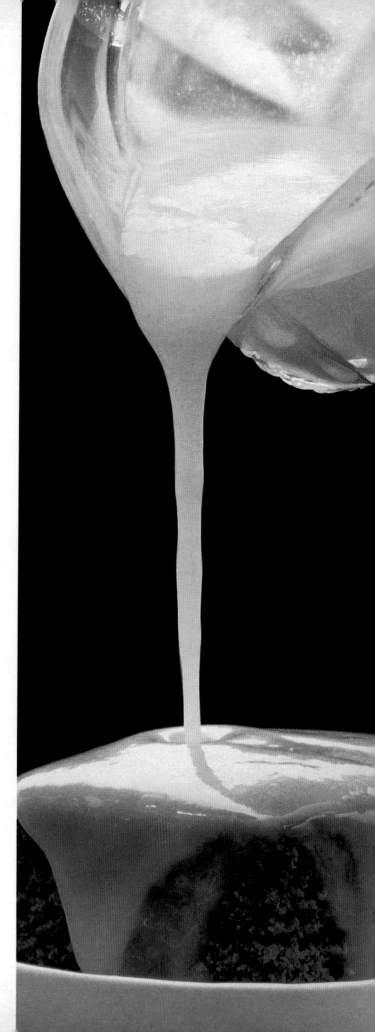

Rocky Road Candy

   1 package (6 ounces) semisweet or milk
       chocolate chips
   2 tablespoons half-and-half
   1 teaspoon vanilla
   2 cups miniature marshmallows
1½ cups chopped nuts
   1 cup shredded coconut

Makes 2 dozen pieces

Combine chocolate chips and half-and-half in medium bowl. Microwave at MEDIUM-HIGH (70%) until chocolate chips are melted, 1 to 3 minutes, stirring once during cooking.

Stir in vanilla and remaining ingredients until coated. Press into greased square baking dish, 8 × 8 inches. Chill. Cut into squares.

Per Serving:			
Calories:	113	Fat:	8 g.
Protein:	2 g.	Cholesterol:	1 mg.
Carbohydrate:	10 g.	Sodium:	4 mg.

Chocolate Bourbon Balls

  ½ cup margarine or butter
4⅓ cups powdered sugar
  1 cup finely chopped nuts
  ¼ cup bourbon
  1 package (6 ounces) milk chocolate chips
  2 tablespoons half-and-half

Makes 3 dozen candies

Place margarine in medium bowl. Microwave at HIGH (100%) until melted, 1 to 2 minutes. Mix in sugar, nuts and bourbon. Refrigerate until firm.

Shape into 1-inch balls. Refrigerate until firm. Combine chocolate chips and half-and-half in small bowl. Microwave at MEDIUM-HIGH (70%) until chocolate chips are melted, ½ to 2 minutes, stirring once or twice. Stir until smooth. Drizzle chocolate over candies. (Reheat chocolate as needed.) Chill.

Per Serving:			
Calories:	117	Fat:	6 g.
Protein:	1 g.	Cholesterol:	1 mg.
Carbohydrate:	14 g.	Sodium:	35 mg.

Fudge

  3 cups semisweet or milk chocolate chips
  1 can (14 ounces) sweetened condensed milk
  ¼ cup margarine or butter
  1 cup chopped walnuts

Makes 2 dozen pieces

Place all ingredients except nuts in large bowl. Microwave at MEDIUM (50%) until chocolate chips are melted, 3 to 5 minutes, stirring once or twice during cooking. Stir in nuts. Pour into well-greased square baking dish, 8 × 8 inches. Refrigerate until set.

Variation: Substitute 1 cup peanut butter chips for 1 cup of the chocolate chips.

Per Serving:			
Calories:	219	Fat:	14 g.
Protein:	3 g.	Cholesterol:	7 mg.
Carbohydrate:	24 g.	Sodium:	49 mg.

Peanut Brittle

1 cup sugar
½ cup light corn syrup
    Dash of salt
1 to 1½ cups shelled raw peanuts
1 tablespoon margarine or butter
1½ teaspoons baking soda
1 teaspoon vanilla

Makes 1 pound,
16 servings

Grease baking sheet heavily. Combine sugar, corn syrup and salt in 3-quart casserole. Stir in peanuts. Microwave at HIGH (100%) until light brown, 6 to 9 minutes, stirring once or twice.

Stir in remaining ingredients until light and foamy. Quickly spread on greased baking sheet. Spread as thin as possible for brittle candy. Cool; break into pieces.

Per Serving:
Calories:	135	Fat:	5 g.
Protein:	2 g.	Cholesterol:	—
Carbohydrate:	22 g.	Sodium:	130 mg.

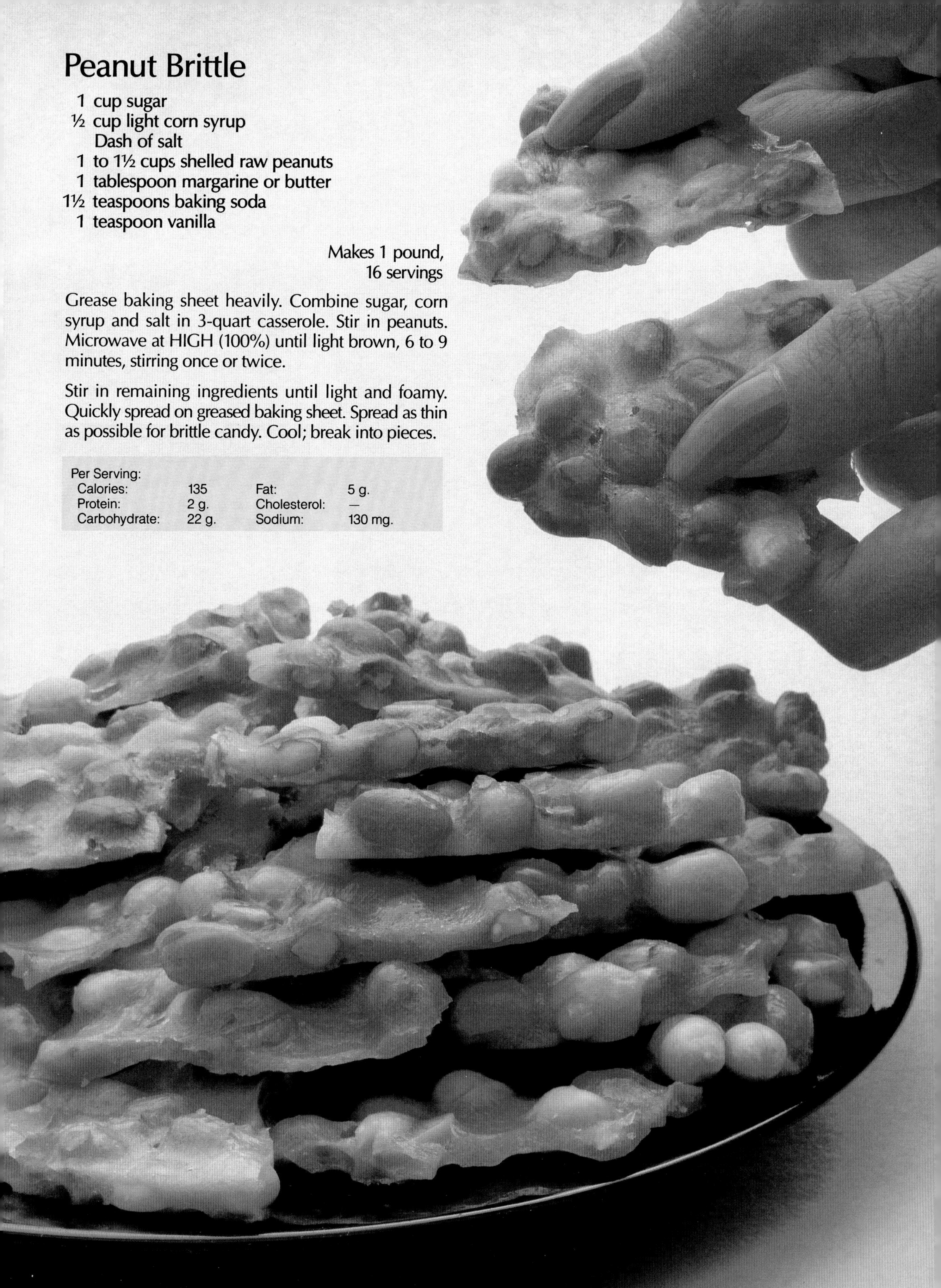

Microwave Tips:
Combine Microwave with Conventional Cooking

Microwave fillings and sauces for crepes you prepare with a crepe maker or skillet.

Soften brown sugar. Place apple slice in bag. Close tightly with string or plastic strip. Microwave at HIGH (100%) until lumps soften, 15 seconds.

Many foods are prepared most efficiently when you do part of the cooking by microwave and part conventionally. Use microwaving for its speed, easy cleanup and for unique jobs that cannot be done conventionally.

Prepare and fill crepes in advance. Refrigerate until serving time, then microwave until hot.

Toast coconut. Spread coconut evenly in 9-inch pie plate. Microwave at HIGH (100%) until golden brown, 3 to 5 minutes, tossing with fork after every minute.

Toast bread conventionally. Prepare sandwiches and microwave to heat fillings and melt cheese.

Warm syrup for pancakes in serving pitcher or uncapped bottle. Reheat leftover pancakes, too.

Plump raisins. Sprinkle 1 or 2 teaspoons of water over fruit. Cover tightly. Microwave at HIGH (100%) 30 seconds to 1 minute.

Brown meats in a Pyroceram® casserole on the conventional range. Microwave to complete cooking, but reduce time by one-fourth to one-third.

Blanch almonds. Microwave 1 cup water until boiling. Add nuts. Microwave at HIGH (100%) 30 seconds. Drain and skin.

Make instant mashed potatoes right in the measuring cup. Place water, butter and salt in 4-cup measure. Microwave until boiling. Add milk to correct measure. Stir in flakes.

Peel tomatoes or peaches easily. Put enough water to cover food in casserole or measuring cup. Microwave until boiling. Drop in food for a few seconds. Peel strips off quickly.

Melt 2 ounces baking chocolate in a plastic cup used to measure shortening. It won't scorch, and you'll save dishwashing. Microwave at MEDIUM (50%) until melted, 2½ to 3½ minutes.

Melt butter for blender hollandaise, basting sauces and frostings for conventional cakes.

Microwave sauces while you cook pasta conventionally. Reheat pasta without flavor loss.

Dissolve gelatin. Sprinkle unflavored gelatin over ¼ cup cold water in 1-cup measure. Let stand 5 minutes. Microwave at HIGH (100%) 30 seconds to 1 minute 15 seconds.

Microwave chicken or ribs until almost done. Finish on the barbecue grill for charcoal flavor. The interior will be fully cooked without over-browning.

Grill extra hamburgers while the coals are hot. Undercook meat slightly and freeze. Defrost and finish by microwaving.

Soften cream cheese directly from the refrigerator. Microwave 3 ounces at HIGH (100%) 10 to 15 seconds; microwave 8 ounces at MEDIUM (50%) 1 to 2 minutes.

Get more juice from lemons. Microwave at HIGH (100%) 30 to 45 seconds before cutting and squeezing.

INDEX

"c" following the page number indicates convection/combination recipe.

　　　　"c" following the page number indicates convection/combination recipe.

"c" following the page number indicates convection/combination recipe.